GW00787327

THE OLIVER TRIGG EXPERIENCE

About the author

Brian Jeeves was born in Rochford on 17th August 1968. His father Anthony first took him to watch football at Southend United's Roots Hall Stadium in the mid 1970's. He has followed the clubs fortunes ever since.

As a writer he has been labelled unconventional, while former Fox Sport presenter Nick Webster once described him as "The Ernest Hemingway of football". Jeeves' first two publications "*Whatever happened to Tina Fillery?*" And "*Airships, Engines and the FA Cup*" have been particularly popular amongst the games more nostalgic followers.

Brian Jeeves is a Premier League, Football League and ECB accredited correspondent for the *Yellow Advertiser* (Covering Southend United, West Ham United, Leyton Orient, Dagenham & Redbridge, Colchester United, Essex County Cricket Club and local non-league football).

He has also made contributions to: *The Football League* webmag preview 2014/15 (Press Association), *Sky Sports, Real Footy Talk, Football.com, Backpass Magazine, My Layer Road* (Matt Hudson & Jim French), *All at Sea* (Southend United Fanzine). *Football League Paper, Non-League Paper, Southend Echo, The Yellow Advertiser, Newham Recorder, Chingford Times, Southend Times, Sport in Essex* (www.sportinessex.com), *Southend Cricket Festival Magazine* and Programme.

As well as that, Jeeves has scribed for the match programmes of: Southend United, Walsall, Accrington Stanley, Luton Town, Canvey Island, Basildon United, Great Wakering Rovers and the virtual match programme produced by The Friends of Clapton FC.

Along with football, Brian is a keen follower of Essex County Cricket Club and has also completed two London Marathons, raising funds for blind and partially sighted children.

A resident of the Essex coastal town of Shoeburyness, he is married to Victoria and has three children, Alfie, Stanley and Oliver. His aspiration is to have a Southend Pier train named after him!

THE OLIVER TRIGG EXPERIENCE

BRIAN JEEVES

SP Shrimper Publishing

First published in Great Britain by Shrimper Publishing 2015

Text © Brian Jeeves 2014/2015

ISBN 978-0-9572352-1-2

All rights reserved. No part of this publication may be reproduced, stored in a retrieval system or transmitted, in any form or by any means – electronic, mechanical, photocopying, recording or otherwise – without the prior permission of the publishers.

Brian Jeeves hereby asserts his right to be identified as the author of this work in accordance with sections 77 and 78 of the Copyright, Designs and Patents Act 1988.

Every effort has been made to ensure that copyright has not been infringed, and apologies are offered should any such infringements have inadvertently occurred.

Book production, design and layout by Nick Snode (npsnode@btinternet.com)
Typeset in Frutiger 57 Condensed, 12/14pt and DIN Condensed Bold
Printed on 100gsm Offset
Printed and bound by 4edge Limited, Hockley, Essex, UK / www.4edge.co.uk

CONTENTS

Foreword 6

Introduction 8

1. Me
Tales of a footballaholic 12

2. We love you Sarfend, we do!
Play it to me one more time 16
Is that all you take away? 21
30,073 days! 25
There is no such thing as a 'nothing'
   game – life in league 2 30
It's no tea party for indifferent
   Shrimpers 34
All smiles (for now) by the seaside . . 38
Hangin' around Hartlepool 42
Talking cobblers! 47
The night Roots Hall roared! 51
Lowly Shrimpers give Austrian
   champions a mighty scare! 55

3. The Claptonites
A date with destiny 58
Little wonders 62
Family affair settled from the spot . . 66
Fans turn out to support
   Billy & Co. 71

4. Tales, Reports and Players
A united identity crisis! 76
Shrimp currie! 82
An afternoon with Billy Jennings 87

Stubbs and French hit form for
   England 92
Great Wakering get the World Cup
   willies 95
Rod Hull – A footballing tragedy 98
The bucket and spade brigade! 100
Million pound madness! 104
Games without frontiers 108
Great Wakering Rovers
   v Leyton Orient 112
German adventures 115
Paul Reaney
   – Master of disguise! 123

5. Jeevesie's World Cup
World Cup 2014 – Brazil 125
World Cup 2014 – Italy 129
World Cup 2014 – Out of luck
   and low on beer! 133
World Cup 2014
   – England hung out to dry 137
Super Mario
   (Stan's first headline) 142

6. Football poetry and verse
A working man's game 147
The Grim Chairman
   – Football reaper 149
Post Office field of dreams 151
We'll never walk alone! 153

FOREWORD

by Roy McDonough

THE OLIVER TRIGG EXPERIENCE really is a great read. In fact some of the tales take me on a trip down Memory Lane to my own playing days.

Brian writes from the heart and with complete honesty, something I believe is unfortunately clearly lacking in the modern day game.

Some great reflective stories including references to his dad who was quite clearly his hero, as was my father. Sadly though, perhaps we don't realise it at the time.

A highly recommended this book, written by a very up and coming football correspondent who is now living his dream.

As well as sharing his stories and reports, Brian has used this book to help raise funds and awareness for the charity organisation 'Homeless FA' who use football to give everyone experiencing homelessness in England the opportunity to develop their skills and abilities, gain self-respect and confidence, improve their health, and ultimately positively transform his or her life. They also support all programmes that use football as a means of improving the lives of people experiencing homelessness in England.

I hope people enjoy the stories as much as I do. You've done a great job Brian you should be very proud. Much like Red Card Roy, which isn't a bad book either! Sorry about the plug.

Roy McDonough in action for Colchester United.

INTRODUCTION

ABOUT 300 YARDS from the very place I sit compiling much of this book, and indeed my previous two publications, is the final resting place of Oliver Trigg.

My father aside, Oliver Trigg, without him knowing, was possibly the biggest influence in my life. Thanks to him, along with directors Charles Stein, George Hogsflesh, Frederick England and the wonderfully named Tom Tidy, I have spent the past 40-odd years riding the emotional roller coaster that is Southend United.

Oliver Trigg's grave

Trigg, landlord of the Blue Boar public house in Victoria Avenue, was appointed the clubs inaugural chairman when the club were founded in that very hostelry on May 19th 1906, and indeed, performed the kick-off ceremony at the Shrimpers opening match, a contest between the Blues 'A' and 'B' teams at the original Roots Hall ground.

Unquestionably, Trigg kept the fledgling club afloat during those early years, indeed, when the Blues were teetering on the brink financially, he donated the princely sum of £861 to steady the ship.

Oliver Trigg passed away on the February 25th 1919, shortly before Southend United became members of the Football League, and in the same years that another notable local club close to my heart, Great Wakering Rovers, were formed.

Of course, what with my father's love of the beautiful game which I've documented in my previous books, I don't think there's beyond a reasonable doubt that football would have played some part in my life. However, the scale would have been substantially smaller had it not been for the actions of Trigg and Co. Not only did they formulate the club, they influenced generations and gave the Essex Riviera something the people could identify with, something that for me and thousands of others has been a way of life.

All these years on from my early football experiences, standing on the South Bank terrace at Roots Hall with Dad, I have gone on to travel to some wonderful places, watch some terrific footballers, and meet some amazing people from all over the world.

During the time that has elapsed while writing these tales, some friendships have blossomed while others sadly faded. Some opinions and thoughts have altered. Time, and indeed football, doesn't stand still, but my appetite for the game remains the same.

No doubt there are people reading this book who support other teams, West Ham United, Walsall, Colchester United or perhaps even Clapton. You'll each have your own Oliver Trigg, someone who set the ball rolling at your respective football clubs, but I dedicate the title of this book to ours.

Of course there are a number of people who have once again offered their help and support. My wife Victoria, children Alfie, Stanley and Oliver and mum Eileen, are my absolute world, they have given me the strength, love and belief to make this, and my other books possible.

My publisher Dave Goody along with the unparalleled talents of Nick Snode and Matt Bann, have made this publication possible, I can't thank them enough. Also, my wordsmith Helen Mulley. Helen has been a fantastic help since I started scribing my thoughts on football. Not only do I count her as a good friend but also as one of my favourite musicians.

Enjoying a pint with John Vickery in the Blue Boar.

Former Southend, Colchester and Walsall striker Roy McDonough once made my all-time favourite team. He has a bloody good book and best-seller out of his own in the shape of 'Red card Roy', I'm delighted and honoured that he has agreed to write the foreword for me.

A special mention must go to Mick Ferris, Nick Webster, James Colasanti and Bill Songhurst, who have shown faith in me and offered excellent advice along the way.

Then there is the magnificently supportive clubs and people who have contributed in some way, however large or small. Therefore my thanks go out to Southend United, Leyton Orient, Colchester United, Walsall, Great Wakering Rovers, Clapton, Matt Hudson, Mark Edwards, Jo Denton, Gerry Smith, Billy Wise, Zoe Newson, Scott Peters, Matt Hudson, Nicola Stott, Peter Dudley, Paul Marshall, James Edwards, Billy Jennings, Sue Darling, Adrian Lowe and Simon Twinn.

I hope you enjoy reading this collection of my footballing tales, reports and poems. Once again, I have added some bits from age-old programmes to reminisce. I have had so much pleasure whilst gleaning these experiences that I'll be donating a percentage of all pre-ordered copies of this book to Homeless FA, a part of Centrepoint, the UK's leading youth homelessness charity.

Thank you for your support, enjoy your football… oh and cheers Oliver, Dad and the beautiful game.

Brian Jeeves x

TALES OF A FOOTBALLAHOLIC

Tuesday 30th April 2013, 7.44pm

"**G**OOD EVENING, my name is Brian Jeeves and I'm a footballaholic, it has been four days since my last game and I'm here simply because I'm beyond help!"

Yep, the dust had barely settled on Southend United's headbangingly (is that really a word?) frustrating season and already I'm craving the beautiful game, and for that matter, any game! Fortunately, the squally winter has resulted in a backlog of fixtures for our local non-league clubs. Therefore, instead of settling back on the sofa with a beer for the Champions League semi-final between Real Madrid and Borussia Dortmund, I am quenched my insatiable football thirst by travelling to the suburbs of the White Stiletto Acropolis (also known as Basildon) to see Bowers & Pitsea take on Southend Manor in the murky world of the Essex Senior League.

On arrival at the Len Salmon Stadium, I discover that I'm not alone. A hardy bunch numbering 47 have sort footballing solace at tonight's low-key encounter. Bowers have always been a friendly club, and tonight is no exception. Stadium announcer Julia and her husband Paul offer me a warm welcome with the promise of tea and biscuits at half time and as many sandwiches and sausage rolls as I can physically consume in the meantime.

In fairness, I don't think either of tonight's teams will look back at their league campaign with any real satisfaction. Manor, never really reached the standards they set a year ago in both the league and most notably the FA Cup, whereas for Bowers, an impressive run to the League Cup Final, has made up for some wretched domestic form.

Manor enjoys the brighter start. Talismanic front man Gary Paterson fires a warning of what's to come when his shot flashes across the face of the home sides' goal. Then the same player cuts in from the left before dispatching a thundering right foot drive beyond Michael Doyle in the Bowers goal. It's a honey of a strike from a player who at first glimpse seems to have enjoyed a pint and curry too many. Nevertheless, Pato always seems to come up with the quickest route to goal, personally, I'm surprised the big target man hasn't had an opportunity to display his talents at a much higher level.

At Bowers & Pitsea FC ground

Before Bowers can rally, their troubles deepen. Doyle's misjudgment of a big 'doff' forward presents Mark Session with the simple task of walking the ball into the unguarded rigging, 2-0 to the visitors with barely fifteen minutes played.

Bowers are clearly shell-shocked; nevertheless, Callum Leahy and 'Manni' Mtangadura are yet to chuck in the towel. Their busy displays epitomize footballers playing for a cup final shirt, Manor might be in control, but these boys are determined to make them work up a sweat for the points.

The visitors continue to create the bulk of the chances. Paterson found Doyle's midriff with another lengthy effort while David Tubbs fired wide after racing clear.

Manor were now leading their hosts a merry dance. Jamie Salmon produced a 'Shane Warne' of a delivery with a free kick from the left. The backpedalling Doyle was in trouble 'Mike Gatting style' as the ball viciously twisted over him and found the net via the upright.

Three goals in arrears, Bowers finally warmed the fingers of Manor custodian Adam Seal when Leahy let fly from fully twenty-five yards, but as the home side desperately struggled to keep their heads above water, Manor continued to manufacture wave after wave of attacks.

After Paterson and Salmon had gone close, David Tubbs drew an exceptional save out of Doyle who tipped his goal bound header onto the bar with an acrobatic leap.

To their enormous credit, the home support amongst the sparse gathering continued to offer cries of encouragement to their beleaguered charges. Although one particular chap, who sat close by, has spent more time chewing the fat over whether to take the burger or hotdog option with his cuppa. As the whistle sounded for half time, he is seemingly no nearer a clear-cut decision!

Julia and Paul invite me to the boardroom during the interval, a mug of hot steamy char and a clutch of chocolate bickies are thrust into my mitts, what clubs such as Bowers & Pitsea lack in grandeur, they more than make up for with a hospitable reception.

The home side start the second period with a little more vigor; the tackles are coming in thick 'n' fast and a sense of urgency has emerged in their general all-round play. However, before they can make any real headway, the visitors strike again. Jamie Matthews whips in a flag kick towards the head of Ash Pibworth who in turn floats in like the proverbial butterfly and stings like, well, a big stingy thing!

The Seasider's are rampant! Terry Griffiths produces the footballing equivalent of a waltz through the Bowers rearguard, before finishing the dance with an exquisite chip over Doyle from an acute angle.

The home crowd are still in a humorous mood, "To be honest, I'd take a draw now," I hear one stand dweller say!

Bowers have the final opportunity of the evening, Mtangadura firing disappointingly wayward with a clear sight of goal. Despite being a somewhat one-sided affair, the game had been played in good spirit and was excellently officiated. I'm suitably impressed as I've seen some mind bogglingly bad whistlers at Football League level this season.

I depart the ground content with my evenings 'fix'. Doing a 40-mile round trip to take in a match, chasms below the professional game, would suggest that my addiction for football is out of control, but it's not like that …I could give it up if I wanted to… honest, I could …couldn't I?

Bowers & Pitsea; M Doyle, Thoma, Gladen, Cris Leahy, Mtangadura, Callum Leahy, Falaise, Tapley, Wilson, Allen, Collins.

Substitutes; Clarke, Blackwell, Chapman, J Doyle, Franklin.

Southend Manor; Seal, East, Matthews, Griffiths, Vaughan, Salmon, Pibworth, Tubbs, Paterson, Sisson.

Substitutes; Jude, Ivie, Jarrett, Kemp, Smith.

Attendance; 47.

We love you Sarfend, we do!

PLAY IT TO ME ONE MORE TIME

*League Two –
Saturday 20th December 2003*

Southend United 0
Bristol Rovers 1

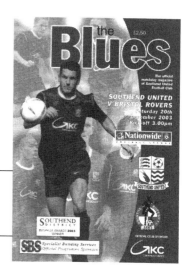

AT FIRST GLANCE, it would seem quite odd to followers of both the Shrimpers and Gas Heads how this docile affair could possibly register as my most memorable match. Neither club was setting the world alight, nor was there anything too out of the ordinary about Southend frustratingly losing at home. Nevertheless, the events of that fateful afternoon one Saturday before Christmas will be etched in my mind eternally.

To that point, Southend United had endured a dire season. The club were second from bottom in the Football League, and had shown little sign of any upward movement.

I was joined at the match by customary sidekick Ed and my dad. The old man had been under the weather of late; the hospital was about to carry out some tests. However unappealing a meeting of two lowly League 2 clubs might sound, he was looking forward to getting out of the house and briefly taking his mind off it all.

We parked the car at Prittlewell railway station and took the short walk to Roots Hall Stadium. It was clear that Dad was struggling a little but he was in good form. "Can you walk alongside me?," he asked Ed.

"Are you struggling Tony?," Ed asked inquisitively.

"No, I just don't want the passing cars to splash me," he responded.

Dad went on to tell us about the procedure the hospital was to undertake upon him, in the way only an old man could.

"They're gonna put a camera inside me," he told us.

"Ain't you worried?" Ed asked curiously.

"I'm not worried about the camera, but concerned about the camera crew," he jovially replied.

After a quick pint, we took our seats in the East Stand, just behind the visitors' dugout. Already something was peculiar about the encounter. Both teams were playing in 'away' kits. Rovers a black and yellow number, while Southend bizarrely sported a 'post-box red' shirt.

Dad took a bag of humbugs out of his coat pocket. We looked at him expectantly as he unwrapped one of the sweets and popped it in his mouth. "I would give you one, but I've only got sixteen left," he said, and returning the bag to his pocket, we could see the tight-fisted old git meant it, too!

Southend started brightly, but after a couple of early chances had gone begging, Bristol Rovers midfielder Dave Savage beat Shrimpers goalkeeper Daryl Flahaven, following good work from Wayne Carlisle and Lewis Haldane, to fire the visitors ahead. Bloody typical!

Southend huffed and puffed, but continued to dominate without making too much headway. After 24 minutes, they were presented with a glorious opportunity. Goal scorer Savage fouled Tes Bramble and whistler Keith Hill had no hesitation in pointing to the penalty spot. Up stepped Mark Gower, unfortunately his truly awful spot kick was easily rebuffed by Rovers keeper Kevin Miller, prompting an exclamation of, "Your mother could have hit that harder," from the old man.

The half time cuppa went down well on what was a cold blustery day. As we supped on the steaming brew, the old man waxed lyrical about the past. I can't remember what anecdote the old boy selected for our interval entertainment, but I'm sure it started with, "Have I ever told you about," and ended with, "I saw him play at West Ham," – and I've no doubt he'd told us it at least 100 times before.

Southend continued to dominate during the second period. As the game ebbed, but hardly flowed, I found myself nervously fiddling with my mobile phone. Despite our, "nothing gets in the way of football," rule, I had met this girl from the West Midlands a couple of weeks previously. I was 'head over heels' and desperate to hear her voice, as I had not seen her for several days. Much to Ed's dismay, I called her as the match proceeded in front of us. The old man was inquisitive as to who it was.

"Just a girl I know," I answered sketchily. I should have been more informative about the recipient of my call. After standing by me through several disastrous relationships, and indeed being my 'rock' through a divorce, it will always pain me that I did not explain in more detail how special she was, and more, to Dad – because he would never get to meet her.

As the game approached its conclusion, Southend were awarded another penalty. Rovers' defender Christian Edwards handled, and to add insult to injury was sent off for his second booking of the afternoon. Regrettably, but as a Southend supporter perhaps not surprisingly, lightening was about to strike twice. Drew Broughton's penalty troubled the ball boys more so than Rovers custodian Miller and another chance had gone West, although thinking back, perhaps it was more North-East!

Rovers held firm to secure the points. The final whistle drew the usual chorus of booing from the disgruntled home crowd; however, today this was coupled with a quite extraordinary incident. As we got up from our seats, one of the Bristol Rovers entourage, whom we believed to be the physiotherapist, began to make what could only be described as obscene gestures in our general direction. Now Ed does not need a second invitation to have a pop back. Already somewhat pissed off that Southend had managed to annihilate another opportunity to pull themselves away from the foot of the league, he suggested in no uncertain terms that both the physio, and for that matter anyone out there from West of Reading, should, "go forth and multiply," preferably in the general direction of Wales. Unfortunately, local 'Bobby' PC Dickie Spooner oversaw this. I recall Dad asking me, "Where's Ed," as I pointed at him being frogmarched along the cinder track and out of the ground. This was something of an achievement, even by Ed's standards, as I had never seen someone thrown out of a football match after it had already finished!

We met up with a dishevelled Ed outside the stadium and walked back to the car, trying to piece together what had gone wrong, and as ever failing to come up with any conclusive answers.

Southend's next match was on Boxing Day away at Cambridge United. A goal from Leon Constantine would secure three precious points and spearhead a scramble away from the foot of the football league. I had a ticket for that festive fixture but never made it to the Abbey Stadium. At around 10pm on Christmas Day, Dad's heart called time and our lives changed forever.

Southend United eased clear of the relegation zone. They would also reach the LDV Van's Final at Cardiff's Millennium Stadium, although there would be no fairy tale finish as the Shrimpers first major cup final ended in a disappointing 2-0 defeat to Blackpool. Things did improve for the club though, and indeed me. Two successive promotions and memorable cup-ties with Manchester United, Tottenham Hotspur and Chelsea.

Meanwhile, remember that phone call? Well, I married Victoria, and 11 years on we now have three beautiful children – Alfie, Stanley and Oliver, who attend football with me every week.

However, throughout those highs and more recently, once again lows, something or should I say someone is missing. How the kids would have loved his stories about playing for Clapton, Ernie Gregory, and sitting on the railway bridge watching Leytonstone. We heard them all that afternoon as we did every time Dad accompanied us to a match.

Bristol Rovers' victory on 20th December 2003 was unremarkable to the vast majority of the 3,771 crowd at Roots Hall... but how I would love to relive that day, just one more time.

Southend United: Flahaven, McSweeney (Husbands), Wilson, Hunt (Warren), Cort, Maher, Smith, Gower, Kightly (Broughton), Constantine, Bramble.

Subs not used: Emberson, Jenkins.

Bristol Rovers: Miller, Anderson, Boxall, Edwards, Barrett, Hyde, Savage, Williams (Gilroy), Carlisle, Agogo, Haldane (Quinn).

Subs not used: Clarke, Parker, Austin.

Attendance: 3,771.

IS THAT ALL YOU TAKE AWAY?

On 7th April 2013, 32,000 Southenders descended
upon Wembley Stadium.

Brian recalls an away day when things were very different!

Hastings 0-1 Southend

TIMES WERE TOUGH at Southend United. In May 1984, the club suffered
relegation to the Fourth Division, crowds were down, funds were tight and
the team were, to this day, the worst Shrimpers team I've ever seen.

Still, ever the optimist, yours truly could not wait for the new season to get
under way. A visit to Layer Road on the opening day of the season had Blues
supporters' pulses racing, but before that, a busy pre-season schedule and a
fixture that took my eye above all the others. Hastings United v Southend
United might not have many people licking their lips in anticipation,
nevertheless to me, visiting a new ground to play unusual opponents would
always prove to be too tempting.

Saturday 11th August 1984. I took the train down to the south coast, arriving
in Hastings early. With time on my side, I chose to skip any form of public
transport to the ground. I would have plenty of time to make my way by
Shanks's pony, and save myself a few shekels to boot. On reaching Hastings
United's Pilot Field ground there were still some three hours until kick-off.

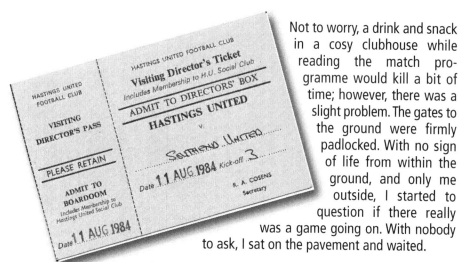

Not to worry, a drink and snack in a cosy clubhouse while reading the match programme would kill a bit of time; however, there was a slight problem. The gates to the ground were firmly padlocked. With no sign of life from within the ground, and only me outside, I started to question if there really was a game going on. With nobody to ask, I sat on the pavement and waited.

I was about to give up and head for home when after about an hour, a minibus containing the Southend players pulled up. Not a moment too soon either, I think one or two passers-by thought I was some kind of homeless vagabond, one woman even uttered "shocking" as she walked passed me shaking her head!

The first player off the old battered vehicle was goalkeeper John Keeley. "I can't believe you've come down here for this!" he shouted across at me. In truth, I had not given it much thought. Southend United were playing and I wanted to be there, simple!

A man finally emerged from within the ground, to unlock the gates and let us in. Keeley told me to wait at the turnstile and he would get me a complementary ticket, which he duly did. I took my seat in the stand and the game began. I started to scour the terraces for a familiar face but all to no avail. It suddenly struck me that I was the only Southend United supporter that had bothered to attend the game!

I actually felt quite proud of myself. Whether it be the youthful exuberance of a 15-year-old Jeeves or simply feeling full of my own self-importance what with being the only away fan, but I began to over enthusiastically bellow encouragement every time Southend so much as got close to the Hastings penalty area. What with this being little more than a glorified kick-about a few strange glances came my way from the locals, probably suspecting I suffered from some kind of mental illness.

Neither the club or the local paper sent anyone to cover the match, therefore I guess I could offer a rose-tinted match report, albeit three decades late. However, in truth the game was largely uneventful. Southend youngster Eddie Patterson scored the only goal late on with a close range header, which was met with a 'Cup Final' style celebration from the Shrimpers singular contingent.

As the players left the field at the final whistle, John Keeley came across and offered me a lift back to Southend on the minibus with the rest of the team. My bulging self-importance was now at red alert danger level. And that showed no signs of diminishing when we stopped on the way home and they bought me fish and chips too!

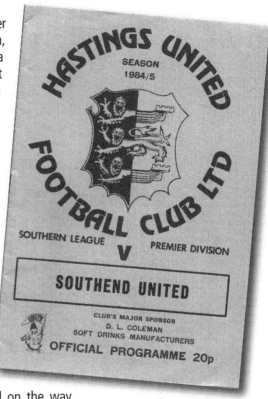

As for the rest of the 1984/85 season, that, for me, was about the highlight. An exciting 3-3 draw at Layer Road on the opening day was followed by a campaign of abject misery. Southend only avoided the indignity of finishing in the re-election zone courtesy of a late Steve Phillips penalty on the final day of the season against bottom placed Torquay United.

John Keeley's turbulent time at Southend soon came to an abrupt end. Somewhat unfairly, he was never accepted by the Roots Hall crowd (probably because he replaced favourite Mervyn Cawston). He finally snapped and walked out at half time during the reserve team's 3-0 defeat at Brentford. Shrimpers striker Roy McDonough took Keeley's place in goal for the second period of that Griffin Park reverse – he told me, "John had a bust up during the break with assistant manager Colin Harper; he showered and fucked off!"

Keeley went on to have successful spells with Brighton and Colchester United as well as with an emerging Canvey Island team. Most recently, he took up the role of goalkeeping coach at Blackburn Rovers having previously undertaken a similar position at Portsmouth.

Eddie Patterson's early promise failed to materialise. Following his release from Roots Hall, Eddie had a few games with Essex Senior League Southend Manor before drifting into the local park leagues. Proof, if ever you needed it, that a career in football doesn't always lead to glamour and riches. I last saw Eddie about 15 years ago in a seafront bookies. He was looking worse for wear and perhaps feeling a bit sorry for himself. It was sad to see someone I'd always believed would make it, in this way. I hope life has treated him better since then.

All these years later a sizable chunk of the town's population, undoubtedly the biggest contingent of fans to travel to a Southend United away match, will descend upon Wembley Stadium for the Johnstone's Paint Trophy Final against Crewe Alexandra, arguably the biggest day in the club's history. Having watched the Shrimpers through thick, thin and thinner, I think I deserve this golden moment for all my troubles. Perhaps, just before kick-off, I'll take a look around at the hordes decked out in blue and white, then sing at the top of my voice "WHERE WERE YOU AT PILOT FIELD?"

30,073 DAYS!

Brian takes a looks at two historic Southend United dates, more than a lifetime apart.

Southend at Wembley

O N SATURDAY 6th December 1930, a meagre crowd of just 1,916 turned out at Wembley Stadium to see a Third Division (South) encounter between Clapton Orient and Southend United.

The O's had been forced to take temporary residence at the national stadium, following an order from the Football League to carry out safety work at their Lea Bridge Road ground, after a complaint from Torquay United about the close proximity of wooden perimeter fencing to the pitch. The Gulls, who'd been beaten by four goals to nil, claimed that the somewhat cosy surroundings had affected their play, and the 'powers that be' agreed. Southend's visit was the second of two league fixtures Orient would stage at Wembley. The first on 22nd November had seen the O's defeat Brentford 3-0 in front of a healthy crowd of 8,319 curious spectators.

As for Southend's inaugural visit, they got off to the best possible start, taking the lead through Emlyn 'Mickey' Jones after twenty-two minutes, however, Orient hit back to claim a less than famous 3-1 victory thanks to goals from Jack Fowler (2) and Reg Tricker.

The Southend Standard reported back...

"A Sorry Display, Southend at Wembley"

Photo © Paul Chesterton

Brian and Oliver at Wembley

Clapton Orient were currently sixteenth and Southend's performance can only be described as ragged, and it was difficult to form any opinion on the new look experimental side, with positional changes and bringing in players from the reserves.

The experienced right-half Tommy Dixon was dropped as was the popular Les Clenshaw, their places being taken by the inexperienced Bob Ward and Joe Johnson.

If the performance against Torquay had been poor this was even worse, Southend persisted with the 'W' formation, which was so well utilised by the Arsenal but not so by the less accomplished Southend forwards.

Perhaps United felt the loneliness of the arena for the pitch was like an oasis in a desert of concrete. In a stadium capable of holding a hundred thousand people, the few hundred seemed lost in the space.

Wembley is famous for an illness known as 'cup-tie nerves' and perhaps there was a touch of it in the foggy air. The dull light did not help matters and despite the referee ordering the changeover to be made without a half time break, the match was finished in a haze and it was difficult to follow the ball.

The score was 1-1 at the changeover, although Orient had done most of the pressing.

In the second half, Clapton was always equal to anything Southend had to offer, a second was added and then the third appeared to be offside, but while the Blues defence were appealing, the Orient man netted.

Southend's smaller, trickier men were no match for the overall bigger taller Clapton players. Southend dropped to sixth in the league.

...and that, for 30,073 days of highest highs, lowest lows, and, er, sometimes even lower lows... was that.

On Sunday 7th April 2013, after a wait of 82 years, 4 months and 1 day, Southend United finally made it back to the home of football. A 3-2 aggregate triumph over Orient – now Leyton of course – secured a Johnstone's Paint Trophy Final meeting with Crewe Alexandra. This would be the club's first Wembley final and it ended a lifetime of hurt and torment for this particular Shrimper.

The Southern Area Final with the O's had been the fifth time I'd seen Southend stand on Wembley's threshold, on each of the previous four occasions the team had choked leaving me wondering if our 'day out' would ever happen. This was made particularly frustrating by the fact that Southend had little trouble reaching showpiece games at Cardiff's Millennium Stadium: three times we had travelled to the Valleys during Wembley's wilderness years.

Nevertheless, Wembley pain went back a lot further for me. My dad, an East Londoner in exile by the seaside, was at West Ham United's 1964 FA Cup Final win over Preston North End. Tales of that triumph were recited to me on a frequent basis. On top of that, as a kid, I had sat in front of the telly every Cup Final day and listened to him say, "I'll take you to Wembley if Southend ever get there." Of course, the old man was smart cookies; always looking to save a quid or two. The tight-fisted old git knew that the Shrimpers didn't have a cat in hell's chance of reaching a major cup final, thus saving him a few bob on a promise he would never have to keep, without having to break my heart in the process.

In fact the nearest we'd come to a father/son visit to the twin towers was when I was about seven years old. The old man had to collect a flat pack greenhouse from the surrounding industrial estate. I agreed to go with him, much in the hope of getting my first glimpse of English football's Mecca. Unfortunately, this came at a cost. Once Dad's aging Ford Anglia had been loaded with his new glasshouse, there was nowhere for me to sit. As a result, I had to spend the two-hour journey home lying on the aging jalopy floor, beneath a clutch of crudely stacked boxes. By the time we arrived back home I was, shall we say, 'more than green around the gills' and all I'd seen of Wembley was a flagpole on top of a largely obscured tower!

Despite not seeing a game at the home of football with Dad, I still had some wonderful memories of going to matches with him. Sadly, by the time Southend chose to end their Wembley exile, he had been gone from this world for almost 10 years.

Crewe v Southend might not have every footballing purist brimming with enthusiasm, so I'll put this into some personal perspective. Since my somewhat deprived Wembley childhood, I have been lucky enough to witness FA Cup Finals, internationals with the likes of Brazil and Germany, and Stuart Pearce dispatching 'that' Euro 96 penalty past Spain before sending shivers down the nation's collective spine with a crescendo of emotions. All memorable occasions but nevertheless, seeing my beloved Shrimpers grace the hallowed turf, well that surpassed the lot.

The 2013 Johnstone's Paint Trophy Final captured the imagination on the Essex Rivera far larger than the Shrimpers' previous visit more than a lifetime ago. Some 32,000 people (out of an attendance of 43,842) travelled from the seaside to say, "I was there"; 26,000 more than would see a run of the mill League Two fixture and three times the capacity of Roots Hall.

There was no fairytale ending to this particular Wembley dream. Goals early in each half from Max Clayton and Luke Murphy gave a decent Crewe side a 2-0 victory. Shrimpers' supporters believed they had ended their mammoth wait for a Wembley goal when Britt Assombalonga found the net, only to be thwarted by an assistant's flag. A poignant moment came in the sixth minute when fans of both clubs gave an emotional minute's applause in memory of the young son of Crewe defender Adam Dugdale. Considering Southend had conceded the first goal only seconds before, this single act of solidarity was living proof that there are times when life is more important than football.

Although I left the home of football disappointed, the day had given me the opportunity to take my children to see Southend United at Wembley, something my father had never been able to do for me. However, just so the old man could keep his promise, I took his photograph and 1964 West Ham rosette so he could in some way spend the historic day at our side.

Southend United 1930; Billy Moore, Jackie French, Dave Robinson, Bob Ward, Joe Wilson, Bill Johnson, Fred Barnett, Emlyn "Mickey" Jones, Jimmy Shankly, Dickie Donoven, Arthur Crompton.

Southend United 2013; Paul Smith, Sean Clohessy, Luke Prosser, Ryan Cresswell, Chris Barker, Kevan Hurst, Bilel Mohsni, Tamika Mkandawire, Anthony Straker, Gavin Tomlin, Britt Assombalonga.

Substitutions: Barker (replaced by Barry Corr 57 minutes) Mohsni (replaced by Ben Reeves 57 minutes Mkandawire (replaced by Freddy Eastwood 77 minutes) Not used; Daniel Bentley, Mark Phillips.

1930 – 2013 TRIVIA

The Clapton Orient v Southend United match in 1930 produced gate receipts of just £100, which would not have covered the cost of TWO highest priced tickets at the 2013 game with Crewe Alexandra (£60 each)!

Clapton Orient player, Rollo Jack, appeared in the 1930 match at Wembley. His brother, David Jack, scored the Stadium's opening goal for Bolton Wanderers during the 1923 'White horse' FA Cup Final against West Ham United. David would go on to manage Southend United, following in the footsteps of their father, Bob Jack, who was the Shrimpers first ever manager following their formation in 1906.

The contingent of Southend supporters who travelled to the 2013 final was higher than the record attendance recorded at Roots Hall Stadium, when Liverpool (0-0) visited in January 1979 (31,033).

The attendance of 1,916 at the 1930 match is believed to be the lowest recorded for a senior fixture played at Wembley.

A version of this story was published in the brilliant retro football magazine Backpass.

THERE IS NO SUCH THING AS A 'NOTHING' GAME – LIFE IN LEAGUE 2

Brian with quill and parchment at Roots Hall Stadium.

Saturday 27th April 2013

Southend United 0-1 Morecambe

THE FINAL SATURDAY of the regular npower League 2 season pitches 11th placed Southend against a Morecambe side five places lower. The fixture is the deadest of dead rubbers with only pride and perhaps a contract for next season at stake.

The final weeks of the campaign have been tough to swallow for the Roots Hall faithful. A season that once promised so much has faded into a sea of nothingness. The highlight, a trip to Wembley for the Johnstone's Paint Trophy Final, has soon been forgotten as the team's poor second half to the season turned positively awful.

As I enter the main entrance to pick up today's team sheet, long standing clubman Ray Davy hands me a copy of the programme from the Shrimpers' 3-2 triumph over Tottenham Hotspur – Gascoigne, Lineker and all – way back in 1989. I comment that days like that are few and far between for those of us

Morecambe fans

embroiled in a love affair with Southend United, but as I glimpse through the aging match day magazine, hope, as ever, springs eternal.

Before the kick-off, Southend's hugely dependable defender Sean Clohessy receives the supporter's player of the year award. Clohessy is out of contract in the summer, fans fear this will be his final appearance in a blue shirt with a host of parties reported to be interested in securing his signature.

Despite a relatively healthy turnout of just over five thousand, the atmosphere around 'The Theatre of Shrimps' is a far cry from that dramatic night when a Wembley berth was secured in dramatic circumstances against local rivals Leyton Orient. Since that passion-filled night, Southend have tasted victory only three times in fourteen matches, all away from Roots Hall. Perhaps unsurprisingly, many are predicting that today will produce another desperate afternoon on the Essex Riviera.

Early exchanges are somewhat 'agricultural' and untidy, with both teams seemingly lost for ideas and happy simply to clear their lines. Southend enjoy slightly the better of possession, but after a quarter of an hour, neither side has created any kind of clear opportunity. Nevertheless, the home side look determined to finish the season on a high, soon defender Ryan Cresswell has a headed effort deflected over while leading marksman Gavin Tomlin has an attempt scrambled off the line.

Tomlin looks in the mood today, after dancing into the visitors box, he forces Morecambe custodian, Barry Roche, into an excellent one-handed save, then striker Barry Corr fires over after sterling work from chief creator Kevan Hurst. Although the home side have the 'bit between their teeth', Corr's wayward effort is met by a collective groan from the crowd. It is an ugly sound that I've become accustomed to after almost forty years of following Southend.

After half an hour, Morecambe finally register an attempt somewhere in the direction of the home side's goal, but the ironic jeers as Andrew Fleming's strike trickles aimlessly wide, should have prepared us for what was to follow. After all, this is Southend United we're talking about; nothing should surprise a Roots Hall regular! Clohessy slips, Fleming pounces, and Southend goalkeeper Paul Smith has to perform his first meaningful task of the afternoon, fishing the ball out of the Shrimpers' net.

At this stage, I could simply throw my head into my hands and scream "I don't believe it!" but I do believe it. This has become a regular occurrence of late, and besides, over the years I have seen a lot worse. As the half draws to a close, the home side look jaded. Passes are going astray and confidence appears to have hit rock bottom. The team trudge off at the interval to a mini chorus of boos and general discontent from the stands. In fairness, it's hardly a crescendo, a sign that at least for this season, the home crowd are almost beyond caring.

At the start of the second period, the Southend support turns its frustrations on referee Rob Lewis. The whistler has made several baffling decisions, but no more than any other official I've seen this season. At least the crowd's fickle finger of blame is now pointing elsewhere, offering the players some respite, however brief.

Southend's efforts have become sporadic. Blues have seen plenty of the ball, but in the final third they turn into the proverbial 'rabbit in the headlights'. Many of us are resigned that once again, this is not going to be our afternoon.

The match has become dull and bogged down in midfield, although the handful of jovial Morecambe fans bring a smile to my face by chanting "ole'" as their charges produce a series of crisp passes that are completely out of context with the previous seventy minutes served up. They follow this up with a chorus of "Bring me sunshine"; they typify supporters in this particular division, often travelling more in hope than expectation, but above all, humorous and bubbling with characters.

As the match, and indeed the season, enters its final fifteen minutes, Morecambe substitute Chris Holroyd finally produces an effort of note, forcing goalkeeper Smith into a decent save low to his right. Southend hit back through Corr, but visiting skipper Will Haining blocks his goal bound strike.

Southend briefly lift the spirits, of the by now largely uninterested crowd, when promising products of the youth set-up Mitchell Pinnock and the wonderfully named Seedy Njie are pitched into the action. Indeed, Njie almost salvages a point for the home side when his late shot is deflected away by the Morecambe rearguard. What a moment that would have been for the Shrimpers fledgling striker!

The final whistle is greeted by more booing from the agitated locals. A season of one incredible high has terminated on a hugely disappointing low. Supporter's stream away from Roots Hall disgruntled and genuinely concerned about the future.

Though slightly disenchanted with what I've seen, this has been a typical mid-table League 2 encounter. Erratic performances, from both the players and officials, offering the audience an abundance of frustration. Wonderful nights like that one against Spurs and similarly when Manchester United, West Ham and Chelsea came calling seem a distant memory, and I wonder when we'll see their likes again. The more cynical amongst you will ask, "why do I bother?" However, this is what I do; it is what I have always done. "Would I rather be anywhere else? YOU MUST BE JOKING!"

Southend United: Paul Smith, Sean Clohessy, Anthony Straker, Ryan Creswell, Freddy Eastwood, Barry Corr, Matthew Lund, Kevan Hurst, Luke Prosser, Ryan Leonard, Gavin Tomlin.

Southend Subs: Daniel Bentley, Mark Phillips, Britt Assombalonga, Marc Laird, Seedy Njie, Mitchell Pinnock, Ryan Auger.

Morecambe: Barry Roche, Robbie Threlfall, Will Haining, Andrew Wright, Lewis Alessandra, Ryan Williams, Stewart Drummond, Andrew Fleming, Joe Mwasile, Andy Parrish, Jack Redshaw.

Morecambe Subs: Andreas Arestidou, Jordan Burrow, Gary McDonald, Joe McGee, Aaron McGowan, Chris Holroyd.

Attendance: 5,081.

IT'S NO TEA PARTY FOR INDIFFERENT SHRIMPERS!

Brian and friends at Melbourne Park

Chelmsford City 1–1 Southend United

IN THE BRILLIANT FOOTBALL FILM, 'My Summer with Des', Neil Morrissey's character Martin states, "It's nice to watch football with lovers and friends," and tonight is no exception. I include lovers, as tonight is Ed's wedding anniversary. For the umpteenth time the big lad is spending this special landmark at a football match while wife Hayley has an evening with full access to the TV controls. Still, I guess she can't complain too much – after all, on one anniversary he did take her to see Southend United Reserves. Along with Ed I am joined at tonight's pre-season delicacy by Jo and her dad Brian along with Andy and Peter, but hey, this is a special night, therefore I am dedicating this tale to the happy couple, Ed and Hayley.

Anyway, Southend United looked to step up the pre-season preparations at Melbourne Park, Chelmsford. Manager Phil Brown revealed that he wanted his starting XI to be up to completing at least seventy-five minutes of this latest practice game, SEVENTY-FIVE MINUTES PHILLIP? As a kid, I remember having kickabouts at the old Post Office field on Ashingdon Road that lasted for 10 hours, WITHOUT STOPPING FOR TEA!

Chelmsford City Football Club are celebrating their 75th anniversary. Personally, I'm delighted the club have reached this milestone and are settled back in the City after several years in exile at Maldon and Billericay. However, for me, their current home will never surpass those glorious Saturdays when Dad and I would watch the morning session at Essex County Cricket Club then pop next door to see Southern League football at the wonderful New Writtle Street Stadium in the afternoon.

Ed with cuppa at Chelmsford

The Shrimpers start in top gear. Only three minutes have elapsed when Anthony Straker bursts clear and unleashes a thundering strike past City keeper Carl Pentney giving the visitors a perfect start.

This, we believe, will be the signal for Southend to push on for a comfortable victory. Indeed, both Ryan Cresswell and John White have headed attempts cleared as pressure on the home goal mounts.

Chelmsford's first sight of goal comes when former Southend man Nicky Nicolau fires just past an upright, while at the other end, Will Atkinson sees his free kick fisted away by Pentney. After City's Sam Long has tested Daniel Bentley with a low drive, Ryan Leonard wastes a glorious opportunity to double the Shrimpers' lead, steering wide from close range after excellent flank play from Atkinson.

Both teams seem to find the bumpy surface a hindrance; as a result, the game becomes somewhat flat. Attention turns to the half time fare, but I give the bacon roll second thoughts after sidekick Ed only awards them a 5/10 rating (6/10 with ketchup). Although food is very much our thought, the Shrimpers' minds once again seem tuned in to adding to their slender lead. Twice Pentney reacts quickly to deny Eastwood and Atkinson but it has to be said, as the half draws to a close the game has become largely uneventful. Minds have once again wandered from the respective charges on display and conversation has turned to Ed's shocking new ringtone while Jo is inquisitive as to where we'll be watching Rugby League after next Good Friday's visit to Rochdale.

The second period gets underway but focus in the stand is now very much on the half time brew, a subtle blend of tea/coffee/hot chocolate and Bovril, which had the taste buds taking cover and the Food Standards Agency alerted!

Southend trialist Don Cowan tries to give the encounter a spark, his clever back heel finds John White but the former Colchester man pulls his shot across the face of goal. Soon after, Anthony Straker comes close to adding to his and Southend's goal tally with a terrific effort that whistles just past an upright. In the meantime, Ed discovers the root of the mystical cuppa issue. A somewhat aging tea bag is mashed into the bottom of the cup and appears to have taken up residence there some time before hot water and a spoonful of coffee paid a visit!

Nevertheless, there is still a football match going on in front of us. Ryan Cresswell should have done better when heading Atkinson's cross high and wide, as should Eastwood who runs out of room and ideas after bursting past the City rearguard. Try as the players might, the game has become so stagnant we've taken to flicking through a copy of the Topical Times Football Annual from the 1969/70 season. As the musky pages are turned, Ed questions whether Ernie Hunt of Coventry City was Cockney rhyming slang, while Andy secretly wishes for a head of hair that would make him look more like Gary Sprake of Leeds and less like Bobby Charlton of Manchester United…

Spirited Chelmsford City have managed to keep their professionally ranked visitors within sight and with four minutes remaining, they deliver the proverbial sting in the tail. Evergreen striker Bertie Brayley has had more clubs than Tiger Woods, but right now the Shrimpers support are cursing that he's turned up at Chelmsford. The former West Ham United, Queen's Park Rangers, Swindon Town, Canvey Island, Heybridge Swifts, Hornchurch (comes up for air), Braintree Town, Billericay Town, Farnborough Town, Thurrock, Aldershot Town, Grays Athletic, Margate (OK, starting to lose the will to live here), Eastleigh, Bishops Stortford, Concord Rangers, Harlow Town, Tooting & Mitcham United, Basildon United and so on… man thumping an unstoppable shot high into the net, although perhaps Bentley will believe he could have done better with the initial cross. In the dying embers of the game, both Eastwood and White have efforts blocked by stand-in keeper Lee Butcher as City holds on for a share of the spoils.

Although some might argue that this is only a friendly, Southend's early displays have been somewhat disappointing. What with all the chopping and changing and uncertainty at Roots Hall, there has only been a ripple of optimism amongst the Roots Hall faithful as the League season looms into the horizon. Following this latest performance, that ripple seems to have turned into a wave of concern.

Chelmsford City: Pentney, Miller, Smith, Davis, Haines, Webb, Long, Lock, Edmans, St Aimie, Nicolau.

Chelmsford City substitutes: Brayley, Cheek, Dawkin, Afori, Spriggs, Butcher.

Southend United: Bentley; White, Cresswell, Phillips, Coker; Leonard (Carrington 72), Laird, Atkinson, Straker; Cowan (Trialist) (Njie 62), Eastwood.

Attendance: 691.

ALL SMILES (for now) BY THE SEASIDE

Brian basking in the glory before the bubble bursts at Roots Hall.

Saturday 3rd August 2013

Southend United 1-0 Plymouth Argyle

W E SHRIMPERS are a notoriously fickle, miserable and grumpy lot, and to be honest we have every reason to be. Most recently, Southend United have been synonymous with financial hardship off the pitch paired with erratic displays on it. Successive relegations saw former Scotland international Paul Sturrock installed as manager. Despite 'Luggy' taking the team within a whisker of promotion and indeed an appearance at Wembley in the Johnstone's Paint Trophy, Phil Brown, a manager with Premiership experience replaced him in the Roots Hall hot seat and is yet to guide the team to a home victory under his leadership. I know what you're thinking: an appearance at Wembley! Supporters of some clubs would give their right arm for some of that. However, we are Southend fans; let me paint you a little picture. If a new striker hasn't filled the onion bag inside ten minutes of his debut, the regular stand dwellers label him a failure – as Chaz and Dave once harmoniously bellowed out, "Gertcha!"

Nevertheless, today is the first day of the new football season and I'm in a joyous mood. It's like my birthday and Christmas all rolled into one. I pull up at

Roots Hall with a fist full of optimism and hope. Despite several disjointed pre-season performances against the likes of Great Wakering, Braintree and Chelmsford, Southend have taken us by surprise this past week. Phil Brown has brought in several decent signings and friendly matches with Queens Park Rangers and a young West Ham team have produced some eye-catching displays. Yes, I'm determined to enjoy the final few hours of blind faith before reality kicks in. I'm feeling good as the Black Knight in Monty Pythons Holy Grail said "I'm (or should that be we're) invincible!"

Anyway, the scene is set and it's perfect. The old ground is bathed in sunshine, well, apart from the cold and dreary West Stand (some might say like its inhabitants). I'm sporting my new replica shirt and I'm joined by a notable crowd of more than 7,000, including an impressive following from Plymouth. This is for real now; we are all in the 'buoyancy zone'. The lively crowd exchange songs, not yet downtrodden by the reality check brought about by the agony of five successive defeats.

Anyway, whistler Rob Lewis gets us underway, and it soon becomes apparent that Southend are the more fluent side. Plymouth look somewhat disjointed as the home team move the ball around confidently. When not in possession, the Shrimpers' charges show energy and commitment, getting in the visitors' faces and generally making sure they have no room to play. After fifteen minutes, all the hard work pays off. Marc Laird charges into the Plymouth penalty area only to see his strike saved by Luke McCormick, but the Argyle keeper and his back line can do little as the ball falls to Barry Corr. The big Irishman steadies himself before poking the ball into the back of the net. Roots Hall erupts.

The goal opens up the game. Plymouth start to find some space, and indeed create a couple of chances. Firstly, the wonderfully named Connor Hourihane finds Andre Blackman, but the Argyle man is forced up a blind alley, then Romauld Boco crosses for Ruben Reid only for the striker to skew his effort well wide.

Although Southend are going about their business with vigour, there is little in the way of clear goal scoring opportunities. In fact, it's Plymouth who have the best chance finding the net. Laird brings down Blackman only for Paul Wotton to fire the resulting free kick tamely at Shrimpers custodian Daniel Bentley.

After the break, Southend step up the tempo. Anthony Straker sees his cross hacked clear while Freddy Eastwood surges down the left before picking out Ryan Leonard, only for the former Plymouth man's shot to be charged down.

The Shrimpers continue to press, Will Atkinson's shot deflected wide, then Eastwood's vicious free-kick awkwardly turned aside by McCormick.

Southend should be out of sight. Argyle give them a timely reminder that they are still in it, though, when Durrell Berry's cross is scrambled clear by Mark Phillips. But it is the home side who continue to have the 'lion's share' in the way of goal attempts. Lairds places the ball low to McCormick's left only for the glovesman to make a brilliant save, and then the otherwise excellent Straker should have done better, firing over from close range.

Until now, Plymouth's team performance clearly hasn't possessed the same passion of the 1,200 voyagers who have vocally backed them. Nonetheless, sensing they could still salvage something from the game, they start to give Southend some anxious moments. Bentley is forced to slice clear Phillip's backpass then the young goalkeeper impressively keeps out Hourihane's low drive showing why Phil Brown tipped him one day to play for England.

Despite the late rally, Southend holds on for a deserved victory. The team leaves the field to a thundering ovation from the approving Roots Hall throng.

I make my way out of Roots Hall amidst a multitude of smiles and contentment. The team have played well, three points are in the bag and I've got fish 'n' chips for tea. I'm going to the pub to enjoy a few beers tonight before the proverbial knee in the knackers otherwise known as 'the rest of the season' kicks in. We have Hartlepool United away next week, and they're bottom of the table, easy, things can't get any better... however, the wife was listening to a programme on BBC Radio 4 the other day. Apparently, one day in the future the sun is going to expand, explode, and engulf our planet thus killing off all life on earth. Depressing, isn't it? Perhaps I'll just stay in and have an early night; typical grouchy Shrimper, HUMBUG!

Southend United: Bentley, White, Phillips, Prosser, Coker, Atkinson, Leonard, Laird, Straker, Eastwood (Reid 68), Corr (Clifford 86).

Southend United substitutes: Smith, Timlin, Reid, Clifford, Bennett, Njie, Payne.

Plymouth Argyle: McCormick, Berry, Hourihane, Alessandra, Boco, Reid (Harvey 71), Morgan, Blizzard (Young 76), Wotton (Richards 45), Nelson, Blackman.

Plymouth Argyle substitutes: Cole, Harvey, Richards, Vassell, Purrington, Young, Lane.

Attendance: 7,044.

HANGIN' AROUND HARTLEPOOL

Brian undertakes a mammoth away day with his beloved Shrimpers.

Saturday 10th August 2013

Hartlepool United 0-1 Southend United

WHY WOULD ANYONE clamber out of bed at 4:57am on a Saturday morning? It's bloody stupid I know. Nonetheless, up and down the country, week after week, hordes of football supporters from different walks of life are falling out of their pit at 'stupid o'clock' in a quest to watch the beautiful game in far flung places – and today it's me.

I creep out of the house careful not to wake the wife and kids and set off to meet sidekick Mark Edwards. 'Ed' has sneaked out of his house too. I'm not sure his wife Hayley was thrilled about our impending adventure, I think she believes I lead him astray, and you don't get too much further astray than a 562-mile round trip to Hartlepool. Somewhat jadedly, we board the 6am Travelzone coach heading for the North-East. The trip is headed up by Paul Marshall aka Wino. Paul, a 47-year-old wood machinist has followed Southend United for donkey's years. He started running coaches to away fixtures believing he could offer fans cheap and efficient travel with entertainment and food thrown in. Shrimpers' fans have responded to this, with more than 800 people using this service during the last campaign. Despite the long trip ahead, it is another full house aboard the Travelzone express today. As the coach reaches its various pick-up points, Phil Cox, a 48-year-old civil servant who hasn't missed a Southend game for 24 years joins us. Phil has often travelled more in hope than expectation and when asked how the match would pan out, he responds, "Is that a trick question?" We are also united with Fred 'senior' and a bloke called Alan who has travelled from Alicante in Spain for our adventure.

Brian and Ed with the Yorkshire Blues flag.

With all collections complete, we hurtle Northwards up the A1, eventually arriving in the picturesque town of Thirsk. The Cross Keys public house warmly welcomes us in with a buffet and good selection of ales, which the travelling Shrimpers put away with gusto. I love pubs like this, old fashioned and homely; it instantly joins my unofficial list of top ten boozers in the world.

Whilst there, we meet up with Simon Twinn, fondly known to Shrimpers fans as 'Yorkshire Blue'. Simon was born in Essex but moved to Yorkshire when he was 12. He recalled taking a fair amount of stick at his new school from kids who followed the likes of Leeds and Middlesbrough, making him feel like the proverbial round peg in a square hole. However, now at the age of 47, he seems to have won the locals round. Many of his friends now look out for Southend United as their second team. I ask him if he feels confident ahead of today's match, he replies with adopted Yorkshire grit, "Yeh, why not, it's the start of the season."

We arrive at the Victoria Ground in good time. Ed and I go in search of a programme and team sheet along with some pre-match grub.

Approaching the entrance, we see a couple of legendary figures of North Eastern football. I miss out on an autograph from former Manchester United and England defender Gary Pallister, but manage to get a photo with Hartlepool's famous mascot H'Angus the Monkey! The tale of H'Angus goes back to the Napoleonic war. A French vessel was shipwrecked off Hartlepool –

legend has it the only survivor picked up was a monkey in a French uniform. Believing it was an enemy spy, the locals held a trial and subsequently hung the poor creature. All these years later, the monkey's myth lives on in the shape of the football club's lucky charm.

As the turnstiles rhythmically click our admission to the ground, I bump into Nicola Stott, an office clerk by day, football and cricket fanatic the rest of the time. Nicola first watched Southend United on New Year's Day 1992, a fond memory as Southend thrashed Newcastle United 4-0. She is a regular on the away coach, and readily admits her support of Southend has cost her a boyfriend or two. After last week's win over Plymouth, she's confident the Shrimpers can make it two out of two, although cautiously adds, "You never know with Southend."

The game starts at a frantic pace with both teams showing intent within the opening minute. Indeed, it is not long before the ball nestles in the onion bag. Only four minutes have been played when Southend's Will Atkinson makes a dash into the Hartlepool box before constructing a chance for Freddy Eastwood. The Shrimpers front man needs no invitation to steer the visitors ahead sending the travelling support into raptures. Led by Scott Peters, the visiting fans burst into a chorus of "Oh Southend we love you". Scott is a 27-year-old cab driver, who is unashamed to confess that Southend United are his life. He can be seen at home games, often shirtless, beating a drum and generally trying to whip up the crowd. Today, he's drumless, but the away contingent follow his lead in trying to rally the boys on the park.

Southend have clearly settled the better; Ben Coker and Anthony Straker continue to cause Hartlepool problems down the left flank while a fired up Eastwood chases and hustles as the home side defends nervously.

Hartlepool are forced into an early change. Ed suggests the announced substitution sounds like a 1970s TV scheduling change: Sweeney is replaced by Walton.

After twenty-four minutes the home side produces their first meaningful effort at goal, however, Shrimpers' custodian Daniel Bentley expertly turns aside James Poole's low strike. Buoyed by this, Hartlepool start to mount pressure. Jonathan Franks effort is hacked away by John White while a thundering shot from Poole is brilliantly turned over by Bentley.

After Eastwood has seen a drive whistle past an upright, Hartlepool gets on with peppering the visitors' goal. Both Bradley Walker and Simon Walton fire wide as 'Pools' struggle to find their range.

Just before the interval, the game ignites by a couple of flash points. Firstly, Walton's robust challenge sparks a melee amongst the players, which strangely results in Pool's Austin going in the book, then within a minute Barry Corr clashes with Jack Baldwin; whistler Mark Brown stuns the visitors, showing the Shrimpers man a red card on the advice of his assistant.

Presumably, both managers use the break to restore calm. Nevertheless, it isn't surprising that Hartlepool, wanting to make the numerical advantage count, start on the front foot.

Brian with H'Angus the monkey.

As the home side probe, the Southend support becomes more vocal in an attempt to lift their charges. The Shrimpers respond by creating an opening of their own. Eastwood's free kick picks out Luke Prosser, but the defender is unable to direct his header towards the target. Meanwhile, Hartlepool threaten through Walker and Christian Burgess, the latter's attempt was greeted with a cry of "I bloody live closer than that!" from Lee 'Mr Pie' Venus in the visitors' stand. Lee received his nickname after finding the back of a Torquay United goalkeeper's head with a steak 'n' kidney pie; this after the custodian in question had goaded us following a Gulls' goal against the Shrimpers.

The home side's efforts become somewhat desperate as time continues to move on against them. Substitute Steve Howard becomes the target of a series of 'doffs' forward, as Hartlepool looks to utilise his aerial presence. Nonetheless, Southend defend resolutely, quite comfortably in fact. The Shrimpers support belt out the tune of *The Great Escape*, but this is no flee from danger, they've stuck to their guns and played some controlled stuff. A shriek from Mr Brown's whistle signals the end of the game. Southend captain John White leads his troops over to the jubilant group who had set off from the Essex Riviera some eleven hours earlier.

The journey home is boisterous. Two victories on the trot have filled us with a bout of early season optimism. Freddy 'senior' has enjoyed his first away day with the Travelzone crew. He holds his phone aloft as the inhabitants of the coach sing the name of our talismanic goal scorer to the recipient of the call, his son Freddy Eastwood.

Our voyage is interrupted with another welcome stop at the Cross Keys where we say farewell to the Yorkshire Blue, followed some way down the road by Peterborough services. It is here that we find our triumphant team. Travelzoners race inside to congratulate our heroes, it's great to see the team respond by posing for pictures and signing autographs. To the untrained eye they are just League Two footballers, to us they are, at least today, gods.

This act of solidarity between players and fans isn't something many Premiership followers will comprehend. The chances of getting anywhere near their cotton wool warriors are almost non-existent, as are the odds on these footballers really giving a monkeys about the throngs who adore them. However, clearly, it's not all allure in the lower leagues, I'll leave the last line to the cashier in W.H. Smiths at the services who told us, "You should have been here ten minutes ago, we had Halifax Town in, they're a right bunch of miserable buggers!"

Hartlepool United: Flinders, Austin, Baldwin, Burgess, Holden, Walker, Franks, Sweeney, Poole, Compton, James.

Hartlepool United subs: Rafferty, Collins, Walton, Howard, Richards, Rodney, Boagey.

Southend United: Bentley, White, Coker, Laird, Phillips, Prosser, Eastwood, Corr, Straker, Atkinson, Leonard.

Southend United subs: P.Smith, Timlin, Reid, Cowan, Clifford, Payne, Thompson.

Attendance: 3,479 – (215 from Southend).

TALKING COBBLERS!

Brian contemplates using earplugs at Roots Hall Stadium.

Saturday 17th August 2013

Southend United 2-0 Northampton Town

THE BEAUTY OF FOOTBALL is that it is a game of opinions. You and I could watch the same match but come up with completely contrasting views. It doesn't mean either of us knows any more or less about the game or indeed the team or players we love, just that we've scrutinised proceedings in a different way. Of course, we pay our money at the turnstile and we are all entitled to our opinions... However, sometimes that entitlement is abused, and I can think of no better example of this than the bloke who sits behind me at fortress Roots Hall.

I write this piece, safe in the knowledge that most of the supporters sitting around me agree. Why he bothers going to football is anyone's guess. Sure, I know Southend United can drive you to the edge, drink and medical help, but when the team are on the crest of a wave you really don't have the right to act like the proverbial bully behind the big fence.

Let us refer to our subject as 'Expert Panellist' as clearly he should join the assemblage of former alcoholics, druggies and failed lower league managers whom we have occasionally seen spouting their verbal diarrhoea on certain Saturday afternoon TV soccer shows. He bellows every thought at ten decibels so everyone can hear him, and believes only his view matters. Already this season he has made idiotic statements of 'Helen Chamberlain' proportions (hardly a favourite amongst Shrimpers fans after her attempt to sabotage our

Stanley getting an autograph off Dan Bentley.

big day at Wembley). First, during a pre-season friendly with Queen's Park Rangers he boldly claimed, "This has nil-nil written all over it" when the score was already 1-1. Then after just two minutes of a Capital One Cup tie with Yeovil Town, he spouted, "So do I," when Glovers followers harmonically chanted how they wanted to go home because of Southend's resemblance to a public toilet. *Don't let me stop you mate, sod off!*

Anyway, football. Southend United have made a decent start to their League Two campaign. Victories over Plymouth and Hartlepool see the Shrimpers sitting pretty in the league, and already tongues are wagging about a possible push for promotion. Nevertheless, this afternoon the bar is raised. Northampton Town are amongst the division's favourites, they arrive on the Essex Riviera in the knowledge it's been almost five years since they've lost here. We get off to a feisty start with a flurry of early yellow cards and a penalty for the Cobblers. Will Atkinson mistimes a challenge on Joe Widdowson, and whistler Mr A. Davies (who is already struggling to control proceedings) points to the spot. From our seats at the far end of the East Stand, it's difficult to tell if the decision is accurate or not; cue Expert Panellist: "You can't tackle like that, penalty all day long" he bawls. He must have bionic eyes to have clearly seen it from here. Anyhow, it's all irrelevant. Southend simply do not concede goals just now. Roy O'Donovan fires his spot kick low to Daniel Bentley's left, only to see the Shrimpers custodian turn it aside with a wonderful save. "Crap penalty," EP scoffs. While the rest of the Roots Hall laud their goalie, he simply cannot bring himself to pass any credit to our heroic future England star.

The game continues in a cagey manor. Southend are playing the more fluent football while Northampton are reliant on brute force to stem the flow. Anthony Straker has made a decent start to the campaign, and once again today is involved in some of Southend's brightest moments. I'm pleased for the lad, he's an honest footballer who has worked hard on his game following a disappointing first season at Roots Hall, something that's completely lost on dear old EP. "Go on Straker, make a name for yourself," he sarcastically calls out every time the Shrimpers wide man receives the ball. This was boring the first time, but now, twenty minutes into proceedings, the urge to ram a rolled up pair of socks into his gob has become somewhat overpowering. Southend break down the left flank, but Straker's cross towards Barry Corr is plucked out of the air by Cobblers custodian Matt Duke. "Rubbish Straker!" EP once again fires unjust abuse at the Southend man; perhaps he was bullied at school or something.

The robust tackling was always going to produce a flash point. Chris Hackett is late on Straker, resulting in a second yellow card for the Cobblers player. "You can get up now Straker," EP spouts at the prostrate Shrimpers man as a beleaguered Hackett trudges off the field.

Despite the numerical disadvantage, Northampton come desperately close to grabbing the lead. Lee Collins' header looks destined for the net only for skipper White to avert the danger in the nick of time.

Then a goal – Freddy Eastwood's strike is deflected into the path of Straker, and to the delight of the home crowd he guides the ball past Duke to give Southend the lead. Well, I say delight of the home crowd, all bar one. "He knew about as much about that as I did," EP yells mockingly. Don't give yourself that much credit, mate, I think to myself.

From the restart, Southend gain possession but a pass from Straker goes wayward in its search for Eastwood. A predictable response of, "If I had a pound for every crap pass you've made Straker," roars out from the seat behind me – please mate, for God's sake buy a season ticket at West Ham!

Southend reach the interval with their lead intact. The crowd warmly applaud the team off the field while EP disappears in the direction of the food bar. If he's this critical of our footballers, Christ alone knows what he'll make of a Roots Hall hotdog!

After the half time brew, Southend set about cementing a third successive league victory. White picks out Corr with a delicious cross, but the Shrimpers front man can't find the target with his header. Northampton rally, but Northern Ireland under 21s defender Adam Thompson reads the situation and snubs out a potential threat. "Well played Atkinson," EP shouts, there is a deathly silence as I dare to correct his wayward identification of one of our own players.

As the home side press, EP continues to get the names mixed up, except for poor old Anthony Straker who continues to shoulder the brunt of his blinkered abuse. I wonder how many games it'll be before this so-called supporter gives the bloke a bit of credit. And I go back to my original line of thinking: probably bullied at school.

Just after the hour mark, the home side seal the points. We long to see the Freddy Eastwood who once captured the imagination of the Roots Hall crowd. Well, now there are signs that he's rediscovered the Midas touch as he latches on to White's path before dispatching a crisp finish beyond Duke to double the lead.

There's still time for Duke to deny both Corr and Atkinson, while Eastwood fires over as Southend threaten to run riot.

A shriek from Mr Davies' whistle confirms Southend's best start to a league campaign for umpteen years. The team are looking unified, indeed it is difficult to single out any particular star man when they are all working together much like the components in a highly tuned engine. Nevertheless, you can't keep everyone happy. "We were a bit lucky at times," EP states, however, to whom is anyone's guess. Anyway, Southend troop off the park sitting level at the top of League Two with Oxford United and I'm safe in the knowledge it'll be three weeks before I have to listen to EP's ramblings again as the next two games are away. I understand from a fellow supporter that our expert regularly performs in local amateur dramatics. I wonder if our Anthony, or for that matter any real supporter, fancies joining me for a season ticket at the Palace Theatre? *"RUBBISH HAMLET!"*

Southend United: Bentley, White, Coker, Laird, Prosser, Eastwood, Corr, Straker, Atkinson, Leonard, Thompson.

Southend United substitutes: P. Smith, Timlin, Reid, Hurst, Cowan, Clifford, Payne.

Northampton Town: Duke, Amankwaah, Widdowson, Carter, Collins, O'Donovan, Hackett, Tozer, Deegan, Emerton, Blythe.

Northampton Town substitutes: Demontagnac, Platt, Morris, Snedker, Hooper, Dias, Tony.

Attendance: 5,510.

THE NIGHT ROOTS HALL ROARED!

Brian recalls a defining moment from his time on the Roots Hall terraces.

Wednesday 10th January 1979

Southend Utd. v. Liverpool

Official programme
F.A. Cup — Third Round
Roots Hall, Sat. Jan. 6, 1979
Kick-off 3 p.m.

25p

Southend United 0-0 Liverpool

S ATURDAY 6TH JANUARY 1979 was to be, up until that point, the most exciting day of my fledgling existence. From the moment Southend United's unsung hero, Andy Polycarpou, dispatched the winner past old adversaries Watford in an FA Cup second round replay, all I talked and indeed thought about was the visit to Roots Hall of European Champions Liverpool.

There was no disputing it, certainly not on the playground at Holt Farm Juniors, or for that matter probably any other school in the surrounding districts. Whatever the 1970s equivalent of Twitter trending was, Southend United were it!

All of a sudden, everyone supported them. West Ham, Arsenal and Spurs scarves were back in the bottom draw. Blue and White adorned the town's shop windows and tickets for the big match were like gold dust. Around thirty thousand punters were expected through the turnstiles, the biggest audience to watch Southend since back in 1956, when Manchester City had somehow withstood a Shrimpers barrage in the Roots Hall mud to steal an undeserved 1-0 victory, largely, I might add, due to the brilliance of Ex-German paratrooper

Bert Trautmann in their goal. However, all that was almost three decades ago. Now cup fever had undoubtedly returned to the Essex Riviera, and to be honest, if you hadn't caught it you must have been living on the moon.

Anyway, despite Roots Hall being embraced with the rare warmth of optimism, a howling northerly wind brought snow to the seaside, and lots of it. Attempts to get the pitch playable were thwarted, thus to my bitter disappointment the game was put back to Wednesday 10th January, now the new day, pencilled in, was to be the most exciting of my life.

The extended wait seemed like a lifetime. Come that fateful day the tension was unbearable. All I could think about in class was Liverpool's unlikely downfall (which made a change from daydreaming about Susan Levitt). Schoolwork and football became scrambled into one (OK, nothing too unusual there), as my overactive mind struggled to cope with it all. As far as I was concerned, at the Battle of Hastings, Kenny Dalglish got an arrow in his eye, 12 x 12 = Graeme Souness and I'm pretty sure that Emlyn Hughes was responsible for starting the Great Fire of London. Four o'clock could not come quick enough!

When it did, Dad was waiting at the school gates for me. Despite there still being three and a half hours until kick-off, we went straight to Roots Hall. By half past four, we were in the ground, along with some five thousand other early birds. We picked a vantage point by the perimeter wall just to the left of the goal on the old South Bank, a huge terrace without a roof. We always stood here, whatever the weather. It was the cheapest part of the ground; the old man was always keen to save a bob or two, even if it meant being soaked, frozen, or both, in the process.

As kick off slowly approached, the crowd built up, as did a clutch of ugly looking snow clouds, directly above Roots Hall. Soon, a flurry had turned into a blizzard. Southend's youth team players were charged with the task of clearing the pitch as best they could while the groundsman repainted lines blue. One of the Shrimpers youngsters, Garry Nelson, was pelted with snowballs after some of his colleagues let slip to the travelling Kopites in the North Bank that he was an Evertonian.

Just before half past seven the wait was over, and not a moment too soon! My fingers and feet were freezing, but the sight of the players running out onto the white covered pitch made me forget all that. The old man held me up on the wall to get a better glimpse of the action – how he managed to keep me there for the whole match is a miracle in itself, a real sign of how heroic a dad can be without being recognised for it.

The snow-covered pitch was a great leveller. Southend largely held their own as the First Division giants struggled to gain any kind of authority. Blues custodian, Mervyn Cawston, was largely untroubled, although I do recall him turning an effort from Dalglish over the bar.

Southend were not to be denied a famous result and a deserved replay at Anfield. Indeed, had the treacherous pitch allowed Shrimpers leading scorer Derrick Parker some composure, perhaps a second game would not have been necessary. Although looking back, perhaps the quick thinking of Liverpool and England goalkeeper Ray Clemence who raced from his goal to hack the ball clear, might well have saved our bacon; I'm not sure we'd have survived had some sixteen thousand stood behind us on the South Bank surged forward to celebrate a Southend goal.

At the final whistle, ever-enthusiastic Shrimpers manager Dave Smith urged the crowd, numbered at a record 31,033, to follow his lead and applaud the team from the pitch, which they did in spades. My body felt numb, probably a mixture of the cold and disbelief that my beloved Southend United, an average Third Division outfit had matched the best team in Europe blow for blow.

I returned to school the next day bursting with pride. The few sceptical kids (probably jealous because they didn't get a ticket) who'd claimed Southend would lose 15-0, were sent packing with their tails between their legs – to me, Southend United were by far the greatest team the world has ever seen.

Liverpool would win the replay by three goals to nil, but Southend were far from disgraced. They had firmly established themselves on the football map. Surely, now the locals would flock to Roots Hall in their droves.

Sadly, it was a map that took almost some 26,000 people off-course. After that incredible night waltzing in the snow with the Champions of Europe, Southend's next home match, a 2-0 triumph over Chesterfield was witnessed by only 4,322. I was there, in my usual spot on the South Bank with Dad, but now our place on that Roots Hall terrace was somewhat more spacious. How soon the fickle faction had forgotten the lads who'd performed so admirably against arguably the best team English football has ever produced.

Southend United; Mervyn Cawston, Micky Stead, Steve Yates, Micky Laverick, Tony Hadley, Alan Moody, Colin Morris, Ronnie Pountney, Derrick Parker, Phil Dudley, Gerry Fell.

Substitute; John Walker.

Liverpool; Ray Clemence, Phil Neal, Emlyn Hughes, Phil Thompson, Ray Kennedy, Alan Hansen, Kenny Dalglish, Jimmy Case, David Fairclough, Terry McDermott, Graeme Souness.

Substitute; Steve Heighway.

Attendance; 31,033.

LOWLY SHRIMPERS GIVE AUSTRIAN CHAMPIONS A MIGHTY SCARE!

Friendly – Sunday 17th February 1985

Southend United 1–2 FK Austria Memphis of Vienna

THE ANNOUNCEMENT that Southend United were to play a prestigious, and yet somewhat bizarre, mid-season friendly against Austrian champions FK Austria Memphis, offered the Shrimpers faithful a moment of brief respite in what had otherwise been a dismal campaign.

Southend were entrenched in the lower echelons of the Football League. Indeed, the 2-1 victory at Stockport County two days previously was only the Blues' ninth triumph in twenty-nine matches.

FK Austria Memphis had travelled over to prepare for a European Cup-tie with Liverpool, due to be played the following month. Seemingly, they believed a kick about with an 'out of sorts' Fourth Division side would be the ideal preparation for a titanic encounter with a club who, at the time were seen as the Rolls Royce of English football!

Trevor Brooking scores for Southend.

The game was set for Sunday 17th February with a bright and breezy 11am kick-off. Nevertheless, the odd start did nothing to hinder the attendance with an above average 2,132 assembling inside Roots Hall. In fact, legendary local football hack Howard Southward described the turnout as 'bumper' in his summary of the match – perhaps in truth this was a sign of how low morale had sunk for the ailing club.

Prior to the game Southend announced that a couple of high profile guests would bolster their ranks. Tottenham Hotspur agreed to send Argentinean star from 1978 Osvaldo Ardiles, while the Shrimpers' own World Cup winner, manager Bobby Moore, managed to coax former West Ham United legend Trevor Brooking out of retirement to pull on a blue shirt for the club he later confessed to have "always looked out for".

Brooking's appearance was met with a great deal of interest in the neighbourhood. Sadly, for those of us of a Southend United persuasion, the town boasts more Hammers fans than that of the local club. The former England legend had already been elevated to honorary status by followers of the East End club, long before the sovereign saw fit to offer him a CBE.

On that bitterly cold Sunday morning, supporters arrived at Roots Hall to discover there had been a late change to the Shrimpers line-up. Tottenham deemed Ardiles unfit to play, in his place sending the somewhat less elegant Graham Roberts.

Austria Memphis were clearly anxious about the icy conditions as their players peculiarly chose to wear tracksuit trousers instead of shorts.

Roberts epitomised Southend's spirited first half performance; undeniably, he seemed to enjoy dishing it out to the Austrian Bundesliga leaders. In fact, a rumour circulated on the terraces that Spurs had agreed with Liverpool to send the no nonsense defender in a bid to rough Memphis up!

Southend continued to make a fist of the encounter; however, their resistance was finally broken when Hungarian International Tilbor Nyilasi opened the scoring just after the hour. Future Austrian star Andreas Ogris added a second after seventy-five minutes, he would go on to get 63 caps for the national side, scoring 11 times.

But the Shrimpers refused to fold. Brooking fired home from close range with ten minutes to go, setting up a grandstand finish. The burning embers of the match saw Memphis hanging on. In fact, only a terrific save from Franz Wohlfart denied Southend's leading marksman Steve Phillips an unlikely equaliser.

TREVOR BROOKING

Both Bobby Moore and Memphis coach Tomas Partis were pleased with the workout. However, despite the feel good factor briefly returning, just 1,536 attended Southend's next home match, a Freight Rover Trophy tie with Millwall.

Liverpool proved to be too strong for FK Austria Memphis. After a 1-1 draw in Vienna, the Reds triumphed 4-1 at Anfield for a 5-2 aggregate. They would go on to reach an ill-fated final staged at the Heysel Stadium, Brussels, losing 1-0 to Juventus in a match remembered only for the sickening scenes of crowd violence that would claim the lives of 39 people. This was without question the darkest time in the history of the English game, with the catastrophe coming just days after a horrific fire at Bradford City's Valley Parade ground that had killed 56 people.

Southend United would continue to struggle. Only a Steve Phillips penalty on the final day of the season saw off bottom of the table Torquay United and saved the Shrimpers from dropping into the dreaded re-election zone. The FK Austria match was one of very few highlights during the 1984/85 season. Nevertheless, it gave me the opportunity to get one over on a few of those local Hammers followers by claiming one of their legendary figures as "Trevor Brooking, of Southend United and England!"

CHAPTER

3 The Claptonites

A DATE WITH DESTINY

Brian 'making history' at the Terrance McMillan Stadium

London APSA 2–4 Clapton

FORGET YOUR WEST HAM'S, Tottenham's and Arsenal's, if it's a real piece of the capital city's football history you want then look no further than the Old Spotted Dog, Upton Lane, Forest Gate.

Yep, Clapton Football Club is special. Not only do they play at the oldest senior ground in London, dating back to 1888, but they also boast a rich history including international players, historic European tours and a clutch of honours. However, why do I have a soft spot for them? Simple, they were my dad's local team; not only did he watch them as a child, but he also turned out for the club's youth and reserve teams under an assumed name so that his step-father didn't find out that he was playing football. During my own childhood, dad and I could often be found at the Dog, watching Clapton in the Isthmian League, pitting their wits against the likes of Leytonstone and Walthamstow Avenue.

Thirty-odd years later and things are very different. The old ground is looking a bit worse for wear and the team are perennial strugglers towards the foot of the Essex Senior League. Not only that, but since those glorious days at the Dog with dad, I have acquired a grim supporters' statistic: I have not seen them win for 29 years.

Pretty bad, huh? Well, it gets worse! I've not seen them win at the Old Spotted Dog for 30 years; yes, I guess I'm the unluckiest follower in Clapton's history.

Of course, the last time I witnessed a victory I was supporting the other side! Clapton's last couple of triumphs with yours truly in attendance were both against my proper team Southend United, and to make matters worse, on both occasions (Essex Senior and Thames side Trophy finals) the Shrimpers fielded their strongest team.

In a huge twist of fate, this week of all weeks, is the anniversary of both victories (or for me, defeats). Clapton are, as ever, at the foot of the table with just one game to play. In short, a victory over local rivals London APSA will lift Clapton off the bottom of the league. There's just one problem; I am going to be there!

London APSA have been in a bit of form of late. Recently they saw off champions Burnham Ramblers and you don't need to be a genius to work out that with 'lucky Jeevesie' in the stands, success is gonna be a tall order. Nonetheless, in a week where my footballing planets appear to be in line with each other, I sense a change in the air.

At a first glance, London APSA's home, the Terrence McMillan Stadium isn't the most inspiring of venues for re-writing history, however, it has a piece of green, a goal at each end, and most importantly, a few hardy souls to share this date with destiny – and as far as I'm concerned, that is all that matters. Even madcap commentator Neil Collins is here along with Leyton Orient's 'terrace drummer' Liam Giles. The scene is set.

The teams line up for the kick-off and already there is drama. A hawk-eyed linesman (that is an assistant referee to all you modern fans) has spotted that a corner flag is missing. Quickly a home official races to address the situation as the phantom flagger waves frantically to inform the whistler.

The weather is worsening; a strong wind has brought in a sporadic rain shower. I question whether the condition might assist the visitors' dogged style, and they certainly have got off to the better start, really good in fact: after just five minutes, Clapton stun APSA and take the lead. A series of crisp passes has created an opening for Ben Lowes, who in turn beats keeper Mark Richardson with a rasping drive, sending the visiting supporters, known as the Clapton Ultras, into raptures. I look at my watch... only 85 minutes to hold on!

London APSA immediately go in search of an equaliser. Geoffrey Ocran has a shot blocked while Saiid Jaffa strikes the outside of an upright. At the other end, Richardson does well to prevent Dave Armstrong from doubling the visitors' lead by saving low to his right.

The Clapton Ultras make up the vast majority of the crowd; they burst into song, "Your ground's too big for you," they croon. That's a bit harsh, I reckon - it's probably too big for all the ESL clubs put together.

As the tea break approaches, I think to myself that the Clapton goal has been under little threat... and at that, Jaffa misses the easiest of opportunities to level the match, and the Ultras burst into a Dexys Midnight Runner medley.

As the players trot off for a cup of half time wisdom, an air of unease comes over me. On the one hand, I'm only 45 minutes from ending the worst run in the history of supporting a football team, on the other... what will be left for me if the record goes?

Anyway, the second period gives me no opportunity to dwell. Amidst the sweeping rain, Clapton set about climbing off the bottom and ending my own personal hell for good measure. Firstly, Lowes makes it 2-0, reacting the quickest after Richardson's parry, then Brandon Martin beats the custodian with a composed finish after racing clear of the APSA rear-guard. For the first time, I witness pitch invasions to celebrate goals at an Essex Senior League match, and the Ultras follow this up with a chorus of "Can we play you every week?"

My air of unease has become a bout of butterflies. A part of the Jeeves' footballing heritage is drawing to a close, and I think how the old man would have enjoyed tonight. But, just when you think it's safe, Clapton remind me what has gone for almost three decades before. Firstly, Jagbir Birring thumps an effort high into the net. 3-1. Surely just a consolation; if it's not going to happen tonight then it never will, I reflect.

Nevertheless, Clapton are determined to make me sweat. Daniel Matthew adds a second for APSA after a great work down the right flank; suddenly the butterflies seem to be kicking my insides with size ten hobnail boots.

As the home side pile on the pressure, the Ultras roar encouragement to their charges. The songs have been somewhat jovial up until this point, but now it is serious. Anyway, remember those footballing planets, well they have just formed a line straighter than a Tony Adams offside trap. Clapton break down the left, and the ball is swept across to the far post where unlikely hero Chris Rothon has raced from his defensive post to put the outcome beyond doubt. Arise my new footballing hero, if I could buy a Clapton shirt right now it would have 'Rothon 2' on the back. Ultras race onto the pitch again, the rain is falling by the bucket load, but nobody cares, my run from hell is over. Chris Rothon's name is now firmly etched into this particular footballing epilogue as a line is drawn under our painful past.

At the final whistle, Clapton players and fans embrace each other and generally celebrate as if they have lifted the World Cup. In some ways, perhaps they have. There is a belief that this wonderful football club has turned a corner and is heading for better times. As for tonight, the football has been entertaining and the crowd have been humorous but above all it has been bloody good fun. I'll leave the last words to the Clapton Ultras, who undoubtedly played a huge part in making this a very special occasion (to the tune of The lion sleeps tonight) *"We're the Clapton the mighty Clapton we're gonna win away..."*

London APSA: Richardson, Hussain, Birring, Appiah, Beaupierre, Adeyemi, Ocran, Jaffa, Kilron, Mauthoor, Ogunwole.

Substitutes: Villota, Matthew, Oppong, Nyanja.

Clapton: Mason, Rothon, Jaffa, Matthews, Lindsay, Greenwood, Bouho, Lowes, Pooley, Armstrong, Martin.

Substitutes: Jones, Woods, Day, Alberto, Moore.

Attendance: 80.

LITTLE WONDERS

Brian reporting on the oldest cup competition in the world with an Olympic hero.

Stanway Rovers 0-1 Clapton

BEST LAID PLANS and all that. This week, I was supposed to be scribing my thoughts on Clapton's Essex Senior League Cup tie with Great Wakering Rovers. However, what with the Tons and Stanway Rovers drawing a blank with their FA Cup extra preliminary Round conundrum, East London has been swapped for the suburbs of Colchester as the latter look to settle the tie once and for all. Nonetheless, when one door closes, another opens. Not only has Saturday's goalless draw at the Old Spotted Dog offered me and trusty footballing companion Ed our first real cup tie of the season, it has also given me the chance to catch up with Paralympian, Zoe Newson.

21-year old Newson qualified for the games after being ranked in the top 8 and taking the only position in the women's under 40kg category.

A Paralympian due to a growth hormone deficiency, Zoe, along with countless other athletes, captured our hearts and imagination during London 2012, where she won the Bronze Medal after equalling a personal best lift of 88kg. She is an inspirational figure as both a sports person and role model. Her stature never seems to have been a hindrance. "The other kids were careful with me at school," she tells me. Indeed, it was during her time at East Bergholt High School that Newson discovered her talent for the weights and joined the Suffolk Spartans. As we talk about her path to Olympic glory, Zoe offers me and Ed an amazing opportunity to hold her precious medal. I take the gong in my hands but refrain from placing it around my neck.

"You earned that honour, I'm not worthy of wearing it," I tell her, although I add that if I had won it, I would never take it off!

Nevertheless, why do we find an Olympic hero at a somewhat underwhelming FA Cup match between two minnows, the vast majority present at May's final, have never heard of? Away from competing, Zoe has a passion for non-league football. She can often be found watching her brothers, Ben and Sam, playing for Heybridge Swifts and Needham Market respectively. Previously, they had turned out for Stanway;

Zoe Newson

as a result, Zoe continues to lend them her support as well. I ask her thoughts on the evening's encounter, "Hope for a Stanway win and don't want the game spoiled by a poor referee," she tells me.

Early exchanges are much as one would have expected. Plenty of honest endeavours, but little in the way of quality as the players struggle with the hard surface. Passes go astray and clear chances are at a premium. The importance of these games, even at this stage, is huge. Prize money of £1,500 can make a big difference, as does the gate money from a bigger than usual crowd.

Stanway Rovers start the game slightly the stronger. Stuart Fergus blasts over, then Hassan Ayrton fires agonisingly across the face of goal after a surging run.

The home side continue to press. Ben Parkin draws a spectacular save our of Clapton's Pepe Diagne while Chris Thomas' headed effort is deflected wide. At the other end, Abs Jarriette's quick feet carve out a chance, which warms the fingers of Luke Banner.

The Rovers rearguard do well to contain the talents of Jarriette and Raphael Duyile while continuing to create the lion's share of the opportunities themselves; although this doesn't stop the travelling Clapton 'Ultras', numbering three, from chanting, "You're not very good," at the home side.

Stanway continue to knock at the door. Diagne saves from Fergus, then the big keeper does well to deny Adam Brotherton twice and Lauris Coggin as the homsters turn the screw. The home side's dominance brings the crowd to life, but they take a collective deep breath as Jarriette's shot flashes narrowly wide after the clever wide man has dashed into the box.

As teams leave the field for a well-earned half time brew, we catch up with Zoe by the tea bar. She's happy with the opening period and singles out Clapton's Diagne and Nick Reap for special praise. Having scribbled Zoe's analysis into my note pad, Ed and I head back to the stand armed with tea and a bacon roll.

Stanway may have enjoyed the better of the first half, but now it's the East Londoners' turn to shine. Reap is snubbed out after being teed up by Jarriette, then Banner races from his goal to save the day and clatter Jarriette in the process. Nevertheless, the balance of power has shifted, and as we approach the hour mark, a golden moment crystallises the tie. Neil Matthews wins possession before sending a dipping 25-yard strike beyond the extended Banner and high into the net. The visitors' celebrations easily match that of any cup final as players mob each other and the 'Clapton 3' stage a mini pitch invasion. Minutes later, Reap has an opportunity to put the tie to bed, but pulls his shot wide, drawing an "Oooo" from the Ultras.

Realising the match is slipping away, Stanway pile forward. Diagne makes a brilliant double save to deny Brotherton and then Coggin. Then after substitute Jake Plane has seen Sam Naylor block his shot, Brotherton and Diagne resume their personal duel, with the keeper once again coming out on top.

It's 'kitchen sink' time for Rovers, with Clapton happy to soak up the pressure and play on the break. Twice the visitors could have put the tie out of reach, firstly Billy Rungay fires over, and then Jarriette is denied by Banner after outfoxing the Rovers backline.

Clapton keeper Diagne has long since claimed any man of the match award. His final save of the evening is his most impressive, foiling Jack Harrington with his fingertips. The home crowd are incensed after Clapton's Dean Bouho clashes heads with Brotherton. Both are treated for cuts, however, Brotherton has to leave the field with a serious facial injury.

The final whistle brings about wild celebrations and another pitch invasion. We catch up with Zoe: "A good game, although perhaps Clapton should have had a man sent off" is her post-match verdict. We also manage to grab a few words with the Clapton Ultras. These guys epitomise the enjoyment of football, they are passionate with a sense of fun thrown in, an ingredient sadly lacking in higher realms of our national game.

Overall, it's been a decent night. A candid FA Cup encounter with an Olympic medallist thrown in, and all for just £6. Now tell me, what Premiership match offers you that value?

Stanway Rovers: Banner, Ince, Blanchette, Fitzgibbon, Ribchester, Parkin, Fergus, Coggin, Thomas, Brotherton, Ayton.

Stanway Rovers substitutes: Plane, Springett, Beecham, Harrington, North, Shankily.

Clapton: Diagne, Naylor, Hughes, Matthews, Greenwood, Tatey, Jarriette, Pooley, Kanjor, Reap, Duyile.

Clapton substitutes: Rungay, Alleyna, Moore, Bouho, Arundel, Boetang.

FAMILY AFFAIR SETTLED FROM THE SPOT

Brian scribes his own thoughts and those of one who couldn't be with us.

Clapton 1–1 Great Wakering Rovers

(Rovers win 3-1 on Penalties)

IT'S BEEN 10-YEARS since the old man passed on to 'football boot hill'. In that time I've watched more than a thousand matches, and wished he could have been with me at every one of them. However, tonight, somewhat more than usual, I wish Dad was by my side.

The scene is set almost perfectly. We are at his old stomping ground, the Old Spotted Dog, watching his former charges Clapton take on the club I, albeit briefly turned out for Great Wakering Rovers in the Essex Senior League Cup. Trusty sidekick Ed and his son James are with me, as is Scott, a fellow Southend United supporter who is new to all this non-league malarkey. Nonetheless, as I said, it is almost perfect. The empty space wherever, that would once have been filled by the old boy, is tonight tugging at my emotions. Clapton and the Rovers were, and indeed still are very dear to us. He would have loved this, even if (as tonight) it meant missing the England game on the telly!

Although it is a damp and dreek night, the Old Spotted Dog looks rustically splendid (that mean's 'wonderful' to non-league fans and 'shit hole' to Premiership followers). I've always felt Dad's presence here; it was his original footballing home. He would have been 77 now, and as Ed will verify, he was losing his memory just before his passing. He could barely remember my name, let alone those of the players! We would have heard all his tales by now, along with, "Not like this in my day" and "Would have been a full house back then" for good measure. While I imagine a spiritual dad waxing lyrical about Clapton and the Old Spotted Dog, I'm mindful that my team in this family affair are the Rovers. I'll be supporting them tonight, however, in keeping with the spirit of the occasion, I'm standing under the scaffold with [the] home crowd. There used to be a stand here, it was where the old man and me used to watch the matches from, fond memories indeed. Then it strikes me, I will scribe this report as if he was still with us!

Before the game, Rovers player-manager Dan Trenkel admitted to me he's looking forward to his first experience of the Scaffold Brigada, aka the Clapton Ultras. "I've heard loads about them and can't wait to see what it's all about" he tells me. The Ultra's do not disappoint either. Rovers players Billy Johnson and Lewis Sparrow are singled out for good natured 'abuse' about their 'footballers' hair styles, while the gaffer himself enjoys a chuckle as they belt out a chorus of "*How shit must you be, you don't pick yourself*" as he stands in the dugout.

Anyway, I'm rambling, football, and we've got a delay. A saggy goal net at the far end of the ground has troubled the inspecting flagsman. Fortunately, the Ultras come to the rescue, loaning a reel of masking tape that is otherwise used for hanging their flags. With the distressed onion bag repaired we can proceed.

Opening exchanges are honest and yet scruffy, as one would expect from a clutch of footballers whose combined yearly income is less than Gareth Bale's pinkie earns in a minute. Clapton probe directly and forcefully for an early opening while the Rovers protect the ball and search for a more cultured build-up, it must be said neither are an easy option on a pitch better suited to growing spuds than playing any form of expansive football.

Gary Paterson sends an effort dangerously across the home side's goal while Craig Greenwood and Nick Read go close for Clapton. The home side continue to press. Rovers' goalie Adam Seal is almost caught out by Abs Jarriette. Lewis Sparrow saved the day, heading clear after the loose ball had fallen kindly to Cory Alleyne. Clapton's positive start is appreciated by the Ultras. They burst into a verse of "The Claptonites" shamelessly lifted from a Desmond Dekker track. I envisage the old boy inquisitively asking, "What they saying?"

Great Wakering had found their feet and assail with vigor. Paterson pulled a shot just past an upright, while Billy Johnson's low drive drew a smart save from Clapton keeper Pepe Diagne. Then Johnson saw another strike fly narrowly wide after being played in by Joe Skeels. Nonetheless, despite the typically sincere non-league approach, the teams disappeared for a half time brew knowing the killer instinct was missing from their respective repertoires.

Clapton emerged from the break looking slightly the sharper. Jarriette scuffed a chance wide while Reiss De Souza headed over after a fine run and cross from Alleyne. The home side went even closer when Seal brilliantly saved Ben Lowes header. Rovers almost opened the scoring when Diagne saved first from Paterson and then bravely as Johnson followed up. It was becoming difficult to see which way the game would swing, however, when Rovers defender Fletcher was adjudged to have fouled Greenwood, whistler Mr. Wells had no hesitation in pointing to the spot. Duyile kept his cool to beat Seal with the resulting kick.

Great Wakering hit back immediately. Nathan Fletcher headed over following a flag kick from the right, then the big defender moved in to head the visitor's level after Diagne punch had failed to clear the danger.

Sensing their team needs some more encouragement; a cry goes up from the home support. "Clapton's red 'n' white". With all due respect to the other Ultras, this is a far sweeter baritone than heard previously. I'm informed our lead vocalist is Eva. She is surely every football mad blokes dream, a woman passionate about the beautiful game. Ed and I converse on how the old man, somewhat set in his ways, would have perceived this scenario. "That's a girl singing," He'd say, "And she's drinking beer from a can," he would add in aged bewilderment.

Rovers look to finish the tie in regulation time. Skeels sent a shot fizzing over the bar then another attempt past a post after a great build up on the right flank. Clapton's chance to prevail fell to Cameroon but he fired wide with Seal stranded.

The extra 30-minutes drew us no near a conclusion. Diagne saved bravely from Paterson while Seal used his feet to deny Alleyne.

After one particular jaunt in the Rovers goalmouth, Defender Lewis Sparrow is vocally encouraged for clearing his lines by appreciative teammates. This time the joke is surely on the Ultras, how has it taken them so long to realise the Rovers have a player known as 'Spazza' in their ranks?

The Old Spotted Dog

A shriek of the whistler concludes 120-minutes football. Our family encounter will have to be settled from the penalty spot. As the players make their way forward one by one, I recalled how Dad would predict the outcome of the resultant kick. "He doesn't look confident," he'd state, usually just before the player in question smashed the ball convincingly into the top corner. I realise this is something I've inherited, unconvincingly predicting, "This bloke will miss" every time one of the gladiators takes the lonely walk forward. As it turns out, Rovers custodian Adam Seal hold's his nerve, keeping out two Clapton penalties while another crashes off an upright, sending the visitors though 3-1.

It has been a long, but enjoyable night, but once again, I find leaving the Old Spotted Dog difficult. I take one last look around the old place before disappearing out the gate and past the sadly disused pub. The four of us amble back to the car, but I sense there is one more with us. No one can see him and he cannot be heard, but I know he's there and I bloody know what he's saying, "They ain't as good as in my day!" – Night Dad – Sleep tight xxx.

Clapton: Diagne, Naylor, Moore, Lowes, Greenwood, De Souza, Duyile, Cameroon, Jarriette, Read, Alleyne.

Clapton substitutes: Bouho, Rungay, Pooley, Coulson, Delovieria.

Great Wakering Rovers: Seal, Pugsley, Read, Artemi, Sparrow, Fletcher, Skeels, Baldwin, Paterson, Hawkins, Johnson.

Rovers substitutes: Trenkel, Kent, Smith, Radley, Hepburn.

Attendance: 34.

FANS TURN OUT TO SUPPORT BILLY & CO

Brian reporting from Mile End Stadium

Essex Senior League

Tower Hamlets 0-0 Clapton

SATURDAY 8TH MARCH 2014. Football's media circus is focused firmly on a Titanic clash in the Smoke this afternoon with all roads leading to West London, but as the hoi polloi (41,598 to be exact) head for Stamford Bridge to see Chelsea duke it out with Tottenham Hotspur, I'm at a London derby with a difference, as Essex Senior League highflyers Tower Hamlets take on Clapton in the shadows of Canary Wharf at the somewhat more tranquil setting of the Mile End Stadium.

Anyway, I say tranquil, but Clapton are in town, and that can only mean one thing, their famous fans the Ultra's. But today, the Tons iconic enthusiasts are here to lend support to much more than their team.

Both clubs are backing Clapton midfielder Billy Wise by using the match to raise awareness and a few quid for his charity, Homeless FA.

Wise is a popular figure amongst the Clapton Ultra's, but in his youth he was standing on the threshold of a promising career with Premiership giants Chelsea. When at 16, his family life imploded, Billy found the pressure too much. He ended up on the streets, seemingly with little to be optimistic about.

Photo © Alam Zaman

Interviewing Billy Wise.

However, salvation was on hand in the shape of the Air Football support group, Wise found a platform and has rebuilt his life and been able to help and inspire others. The programme led to Billy representing England at the 2012 Homeless World Cup in Mexico and then coaching the team at the 2013 Championships in Poland. Nevertheless, despite international recognition and a record crowd for a Tower Hamlets match turning up in support, football doesn't stand on ceremony, Wise is named on the Clapton bench.

Both clubs can feel fairly content with their campaigns to date. Clapton have their best points tally in an absolute age while Tower Hamlets have been in sparking form and still harbour a realistic hope of lifting the ESL title.

Despite our hero of the hour missing from the starting line-up, it's a glorious afternoon and exchanges are bright and breezy. Hamlets Kane Wilson fired wide after Clapton custodian Pepe Diagne had struggled to clear, while Luke Kanjor displays trickery down the right flank for the visitors but Joe Killingback is alive to the situation.

The play is already somewhat stretched. Tower Hamlets believe they should have had the chance to open the scoring, but whistler Peter Wilson wave's away spot kick appeals after Sam Naylor and Luke With tangle, then Steve

Willis perhaps should have done better, firing over from close range after Killingback had delivered. At the other end, James Briggs effort is wayward after the busy midfielder had found himself room for a shot.

The teams continue to probe without penetration. Hamlets scramble clear as Kanjor looked set to pounce, while another centre from Killingback whistles across the goal without troubling Diagne.

Despite the lack of a goal, or Billy Wise, the Ultra's are in fine voice. They call for their champion from the stand, "Billy, oh Billy Wise he runs down the wing for me," they belt out in slightly less than acoustic splendour (probably due to a large intake of Polish lager) to the theme tune of 'Heartbeat'. Back on the greenery Diagne earns his corn, fielding an acrobatic overhead kick from the impressive Killingback.

The second period takes on much the same pattern. Diagne saved brilliantly from Willis, then the Senegalese international denied Wilson as Hamlet continued to press. Clapton respond when Ike Nzurba picked the pocket of Willis before sending a curling effort beyond keeper Robert Hatton but agonisingly past an upright.

With quarter of an hour remaining the crowd get their wish as Billy Wise enters the fray. And straight away he's involved, first combining well with Sam Omojola, and then lashing an effort wide after great wizardry by Peter Moore.

The team's continued to toil, Clapton asked questions of Mr Wilson when Omojola clashed with Stephen Brown, but once again the referee seemed assured in rebuffing penalty claims.

The final stages of the game petered out without further threat, but it didn't dampen the enthusiasm of the bigger than usual Mile End Stadium crowd, indeed a Tower Hamlets record of 195, ensuring Billy's Homeless FA charity somewhere in the region of £400, this included a generous donation from Hamlets. There was a real sense of camaraderie and respect between the clubs, something that would certainly be missing from that other high and mighty derby I mentioned earlier.

I caught up with Billy at the final whistle and found his company completely inspiring. He was understandably delighted with the day's proceedings. "I want to show people who are going through what I did that there is light at the end of the tunnel and that they can achieve anything they want to if they put their minds to it". Wise was also quick to recognise the efforts of Tower Hamlets chairman Mr Mohammed Nurul Hoque, his staff and Neil Day, who has

successfully filled coaching roles at both clubs. They are people who recognised his work and approached him to see if they could help in any way.

Later this year, Wise will be coaching the England team at the Homeless World Cup in Chile, but stresses it's about far more than football. "Football doesn't really come into it," he explained, "It's all about teaching life skills, building confidence and trust through football, it's about you and what you are".

I depart Mile End Stadium feeling enthused by everything that has gone before. Certainly, I've seen better games, but very few where the courage and honesty of a player has moved me. We live in an age where fans idolise the multimillionaires who grace the Premiership. Nonetheless, in the short time we've spoken I have found Billy Wise one of the most inspirational footballers I've ever met.

Tower Hamlets: Robert Hatton, Bradley Ling, Danny Gillard, Steve Willis, Stephen Brown, Jay Taylor, Joe Killingback, Steven Demetriou, Kane Wilson, Billy Hickford, Luke With.

Tower Hamlets substitutes: Reece Morgan, Lee Brown, Mohamed Abdisamad, AJ Olatonbosun.

Clapton: Pepe Diagne, Sam Naylor, Peter Moore, Ben Lowes, Craig Greenwood, Jamie Lyndon, Rafael Duyille, James Briggs, Kofi Billy, Ike Nzurba, Luke Kanjor.

Clapton substitutes: Billy Wise, Justin Maynard, Sam Omojola, Dean Bouho.

Referee: Peter Wilson.

Attendance: 195.

A UNITED IDENTITY CRISIS!

O K, THIS IS DIFFICULT to admit but I have a little confession to make. It was a weak moment in my life, I was easily led, I'm not proud of it but it really wasn't my fault… for a few months I supported Manchester United!

There; I've said it. The bloke who has little time for the modern day money mad Premiership once followed arguably the richest and by far its most successful club ever!

Of course, back then 'Man U' weren't the 'Man U' they are today. It was 1977 and the club had only returned to the top flight a couple of years previously, following English football's most shocking relegation ever.

I was 8 years old; desperately trying to stand out from the hoi polloi and be noticed by the popular kids at Holt Farm School. So far, this had proved to be fruitless. After all I wasn't academically brilliant, and I also had to contend with being a 'five-stone-wringing-wet weakling' with floppy hair, who wore 'Jack Duckworth' prescription glasses. I can tell you, despite growing up during the iconic fashion disaster that was the 1970s, this was not the look to impress your peers, particularly in junior school.

It was perfectly clear that just being plain old 'me' was never going to work. I needed to

do something that would elevate me to elite status in the playground; I needed a role model, a popular kid, a leader of men (well boys). I decided I should look no further than our class superhero, a lad by the name of Adrian Lowe.

Now Adrian was perfect – a good-looking lad who excelled at just about everything. He was top of the class in lessons; all the boys wanted to be like him, all the girls wanted to be with him. There was even a rumour on the playground that he could play the guitar, but most importantly, he was by far the best footballer at Holt Farm School.

Already I was off to good start. My Auntie Trisha had brought me a guitar the previous Christmas in

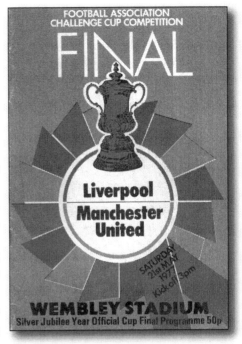

the hope I would someday hook up with her favourites the Rolling Stones – all I had to do now was learn how to play it. Nevertheless, there was something else. Adrian followed Manchester United.

Supporting another club wasn't something to which I'd ever given much thought. Dad took me to Southend United and that was my team. It would be selling my footballing soul but if changing 'Uniteds' would bring me the fame and fortune that was lavished upon Adrian then I was bang up for it (I was particularly eager to impress Susan Levitt, a girl whose smile had simply melted me right from the day I started school). It was all perfectly clear; to get the girl – and for that matter everything that went with being able to get the girl – I needed to be like Adrian.

Despite being far from a good player, I enjoyed football at school, particularly when picked to be in the same team as Adrian. He had recently started to wear the Manchester United away kit during PE, a white number with black stripes running down one side. Needless to say, if I wanted to draw parallels with arguably Holt Farm's greatest ever player then the Manchester United away strip was going to be an essential part of my guise.

Adrian was part of a very good school football team and scored loads of goals too. He wasn't the captain – that honour befell a lad named Stuart Wollard, another excellent player but perhaps a little less flamboyant. I likened them to Gerry Francis and Stan Bowles at Queens Park Rangers. Stuart was Francis, sensible and level headed, while Adrian was Bowles – a crowd pleaser, a match winner! To me, the fact that Adrian was regarded by our teacher as 'too outrageous' to be skipper only increased my desire to emulate him more.

My quest wasn't helped when several other kids started donning the United kit for PE; I began to pester my Dad for the strip more and more.

By May 1977, my badgering of Dad had reached fever pitch. Manchester United had reached the FA Cup final and a few more lads were wearing the strip if I didn't get the kit soon everyone would be like Adrian and where would that leave me?

On May 21st, Manchester United won the FA Cup in front of almost 100,000 people at Wembley Stadium. Final Day had been a bit of a disaster for yours truly. We were just about the only family in our street that still had an old black and white television. The antique set was always on the blink, but ever trying to saving a bob or two, Dad would 'repair' it with a measured blow to its side with the palm of his hand. Up until now this had worked perfectly, but today of all days the set decided to give up the ghost. Dad fought gamely with the ageing piece of equipment, and in the end we managed to see the Wembley showpiece although it looked as if the teams were playing in a snowstorm. At least this distorted view of the Cup Final would persuade the old man that we should move into the modern era and shell out for a brand new colour TV.

Back at Holt Farm School, the Manchester United bandwagon was practically full, standing room only in fact. Knowing all the players' names, reciting the likes of Stepney, Buchan, Greenhoff, Coppell, Pearson (my favourite) and Hill (once incredibly rejected by Southend!), was not going to raise my profile to 'Adrian status' – I needed that kit and bloody fast!

Despite not having the strip in time for United's Cup Final triumph, salvation loomed in the shape of my 9th birthday. Dad had promised me a football kit and I spent hours on end describing in detail the one I wanted. My birthday came amidst wild expectation. Along with the strip, I had asked for a pair of 'Gola' football boots, just like the ones worn by the Holt Farm hero of course, after all, there was no point me going into this identity theft thing half-hearted now, was there? Finally, the big day arrived and I awoke to an intriguing pile of presents.

Rather sadly, I misjudged one small thing, my skinflint Dad! Now I've always suspected I support Southend United because the old boy didn't want to spend a few extra quid to take me to Arsenal, Tottenham or West Ham, not that I'm complaining on that score. Nevertheless, the new TV had clearly put the squeeze on Dad's wallet and opened his eyes to what he believed was a bargain. He ventured to a shop in Southchurch Road, Southend called 'Paul's' – a specialist in all types of school clothing but not the place you're likely to find a brand spanking new Manchester United away strip.

My birthday, August 17th 1977 was overshadowed by events of the previous day. American singer Elvis Presley had (in my eyes, somewhat selfishly) popped his clogs. To my dismay, the family seemed more concerned by his passing than my aging. Nevertheless, in my mixed up little world things were about to get a whole lot worse…

As I tore the paper off my first present, the colour visibly drained from my face. I was not so much disappointed but horrified as staring back at me was a plain red shirt with white collars and cuffs, white shorts and red socks. I looked at dad in a state of advanced bewilderment.

"It's the one Charlton wore!" he exclaimed, referring to Bobby Charlton, the former Red Devils great.

"What? Charlton Athletic?" I sharply responded.

Things soon worsened as I cautiously opened the next gift. Football boots, not 'Gola' but with the word 'Goal' printed on the side in silver letters.

"They've got an extra stripe on 'em, make you kick it harder," he said.

Shaking my head in disbelief and acute disappointment, I ripped the paper from the next parcel. Encouraging start, a sports bag, and it was red! However, on turning it over the final hammer blow struck in what was turning out to be the most shocking birthday of my short existence. Emblazed across the bag was the name no Manchester United supporter, pretend or otherwise wanted to see – LIVERPOOL!

Although the Merseysiders were by far the best team in the country, Europe even, at Holt Farm Junior School that meant very little. United had beaten them in the Cup Final back in May denying them a unique treble having already bagged the European Cup and the First Division title. Being spotted with a Liverpool bag slung over my shoulder would seriously damage my already fragile playground standing even further and was hardly likely to endear me to the almost Masonic circle of friends that surrounded our Adrian.

I pictured myself in the fake kit and boots. In a way, I was a trendsetter, ahead of my time. Retro football shirts are both popular and expensive these days, however, in a school playground back in 1977 they would bring you nothing but humiliation and at worst a 'dead arm' or a knee in the knackers!

The first week back at school after the summer holiday soon arrived along with our first football PE lesson, something by now I feared more than a trip to the dentist. Sure enough, the sight of me in such a cheap excuse for a Manchester United strip and phony boots to match saw me roared at by just about everyone who had boarded the 'Holt Farm United' bandwagon. I tried to fight my corner with Dad's 'Bobby Charlton' line but it was to no avail. I was a laughing stock.

Come Christmas 1977, Dad finally got the message. I received the famed black and white 'United' kit, albeit a size too small for me. The trouble was by the time I wore it for PE it was old hat. The 'fickle factor' had once again invaded the playground, Manchester United were by now firmly in the past, and kids had replaced their love of United with the Rubik's Cube.

I had spectacularly failed at being the new Adrian Lowe, failed to 'woo' Susan Levitt, proved to be a pretty shabby 'plastic Manc', and I still couldn't play the guitar. It was back to being plain old Brian Jeeves, with ill-fitting glasses and a bad haircut, supporting undependable Southend United who'd win when you expected them to lose and er… well… lose all the rest of the time.

Just recently, I traced both Adrian and Susan on Facebook. Unsurprisingly, Adrian is a successful director of a communications company, although perhaps a little bit of me was disappointed he'd not ended up a maverick centre forward with a First Division football club (Premiership to those who believe football was invented 20 years ago by Sky TV) – also it turns out he couldn't play the guitar either!

Susan lives in Yorkshire; she still has the wonderful smile but confessed to me that she is "not much of a football fan". Not even following the biggest club in the world and trying to emulate a Holt Farm soccer legend was going to impress her!

Just before Christmas 2011, my 6-year-old son Alfie returned from school and hit me with some devastating news. In order to be just like his best friend Jack, Alf had decided to start supporting Arsenal.

"Daddy, can you ask Father Christmas to get me the Arsenal kit for Christmas?" he asked.

(The Holt Farm team, Adrian Lowe pictured middle row, third from the left).

I was somewhat dismayed by Alf's bold stance as I'd spent some considerable time and money brainwashing him and his younger brothers Stanley and Oliver into following Southend United. However, thinking back to my own wayward moment back in 1977 I tell Alf, "I'll see what Santa can do," after all. Like father like son… and then again, perhaps I'm like my own father, too. 35 years on, 'Paul's' in Southchurch Road is still going strong. I wonder what line they do in a red and white number?

SHRIMP CURRIE!

THE 70'S AND 80'S was an iconic era on my own personal football timeline. Perhaps that's because of hazy childhood memories or even a stubborn refusal to board a media fuelled bandwagon seemingly hell-bent on urging modern fans to accept greed, disloyalty and cheating as the norm. Nevertheless, to me, back in that golden age the games seemed more exciting and every team had a maverick; you remember the type, shirt outside his shorts, socks rolled down and the ability to run with the ball through a quagmire of a pitch then sink ten pints with a super model on each arm, well, something like that anyway.

Along with George Best, the likes of Frank Worthington, Stanley Bowles and Charlie George were football's equivalent to rock stars. Of course, as a Southend United supporter, the nearest I got to seeing them was on the face of a bubblegum card brought from the corner shop or when Dad gave me special permission to stay up late to watch Match of the Day with him. Nevertheless, I soon built up a portfolio of favourites, one of which was England international, Tony Currie.

Currie, an exciting winger, fitted the bill perfectly, wearing his hair long and displaying all the attributes you would expect from a flamboyant top-flight footballer. After a lightening start to his career at Watford, he enjoyed cult status at Sheffield United and Leeds United. Between 1968 and 1979, he made 415 appearances for the Yorkshire clubs, finding the net 65 times. He was capped 17 times by England during a period when the national side failed to deliver on the global stage, hitting the 'onion bag' 3 times. The total would have been much higher if not for a series of troublesome injuries.

Currie then had a spell with Queens Park Rangers. Despite Rangers Second Division status, they still managed to reach the 1982 FA Cup Final. However, his contribution to the showpiece was to give away a penalty with a 'forwards tackle' from which Glenn Hoddle scored the only goal for Tottenham in a replay; this after the original tie had ended in a 1-1 draw.

With his career in its embers, Currie played in Canada with Toronto Nationals before returning to link up with non-league Chesham United. His time

in the professional game seemed to be at a close, however, a great deal of local interest was expressed when in 1983 it was announced that he would be joining Southend United. And not a moment too soon! Southend were a club in turmoil. The close season had witnessed the club taken over by local businessman Anton Johnson. Long serving manager Dave Smith replaced in the hot seat by former Peterborough United boss player Peter Morris, but as has often been the case at Roots Hall, the new regime didn't reap the riches fans had expected. Morris was already under fire after a disappointing start to the campaign thus Currie's signature was seen by many (including me) as an upturn in the club's fortunes.

Saturday 10th September 1983, attendances were on the slide and Southend in the lower half of the Third Division when Currie was pencilled in for a match against Wimbledon. A crowd some 500 larger than the previous at Roots Hall turned out to welcome their newest recruit. However, just minutes before kick-off, stadium announcer Ian Holmes delivered some breaking news. "There will be a change to the Southend line-up this afternoon, Ron Pountney will replace Tony Currie," he stated.

SOUTHEND UNITED v CAMBRIDGE UNITED
Wednesday 5 October 1983
Kick-Off: 7.30 p.m.

MID-WEEK FOOTBALL LEAGUE

SOUTHEND UNITED		CAMBRIDGE UNITED
John KEELEY	1	Keith BRANAGAN
Mike ANGUS	2	Dave DONALDSON
Dean WELLS	3	Steve CLARK
Glen SKIVINGTON	4	Graham HOWARD
Kirk GAME	5	John COZENS
Warren MAY	6	Keith LOCKHART
Tony CURRIE	7	Lee CARTWRIGHT
Ron POUNTNEY	8	Lee MADDISON
Adrian OWERS	9	Kevin SMITH
Steve TASKER	10	Stephen LYLE
John GYMER	11	Ray NICKLES
John SEADEN	12	
Michael ENGWELL	14	

OFFICIALS
Referee: T D POWELL (Edgware)
Linesmen: R D ERMANS (Chelmsford) - Red Flag
J L EDMONDS (Chelmsford) - Yellow Flag

FORTHCOMING MATCHES AT ROOTS HALL

v AFC BOURNEMOUTH
Mid-Week Football League
Tuesday 11 October 1983
Kick-Off: 7.30 p.m.

v EXETER CITY
Canon League Division 3
Saturday 15 October 1983
Kick-Off: 3.00 p.m.

v ORIENT
Canon League Division 3
Friday 21 October 1983
Kick-Off: 7.30 p.m.

Price 3p

Currie's late withdrawal gave the rumourmongers a field day. Some claimed he had never been fit and that the club had announced he would start the match simply to bolster the crowd; other suggested Currie had pulled out of the game after Southend refused to pay an appearance bonus. Some Blues supporters even claimed he could not play because he was inebriated!

Whatever the reason for Tony Currie's sharp exit, I, like the majority of the 3106 inside Roots Hall, felt pretty deflated. I had believed his arrival would signal a resurgent Southend. It had ended in embarrassment for all concerned!

The match ended in a 1-1 draw with Greg Sheppard scoring for Southend on the stroke of half time after the Dons had taken the lead through Alan Cork two minutes previously. The club informed the local press that Currie had been injured in the pre-match warm-up.

After several weeks on the treatment table, the former England man finally made his Roots Hall bow on October 4th 1983 in a Midweek League fixture against Cambridge United Reserves. His appearance in a Southend shirt brought out a bigger than usual crowd for a second team match, with the teams playing out an entertaining 2-2 draw. His display was steady, as one would expect from a player returning from a spell on the sidelines. Editor Terry Smith scribed in the Shrimpers programme versus Exeter City, that the match was an enjoyable one and added, "Currie's composure and deft touches showed he has lost none of his undoubted class". Sadly, around the hour mark, the injury jinx struck again. He left the pitch to warm applause from the appreciative gathering, all blissfully unaware he would never play for Southend again!

On the 31st October, Peter Morris informed the supporters through his notes in the programme that, "Things did not work as we all would have liked with Tony Currie who has now left us on mutual agreement to pursue his career in other directions". The 6-0 win over Brentford that evening might have briefly glossed over the disappointment of his exit.

Morris wasn't a popular choice as manager with the Roots Hall faithful, and my conversations with one or two players of the time would suggest he didn't have the full support of the dressing room either, but in some ways the beleaguered boss was unlucky. Along with Currie, he brought in some good players including Republic of Ireland goalkeeper Gerry Payton (on loan from Fulham), Ex-Ipswich and England striker Trevor Whymark and Lil Fuccillo, an old First Division campaigner with Luton Town. However, it was all to no avail, a disastrous run of results would lead to Morris and his assistant Colin Harper losing their jobs. Southend could not have gone for higher profile replacements. England's 1966 World Cup winning captain Bobby Moore took the reins with the colourful Malcolm Allison as his sidekick, but the damage was done. Southend only won 10 games and were relegated to the Fourth Division with just 44 points.

Currie did re-appear in the Football League in 1984. Future Southend manager David Webb persuaded him to turn out for Fourth Division Torquay United where he played 16 games, finding the net once. Later that year he linked up with Stockport County but never lined up in a competitive match, before drifting into non-league football.

In 1988, Currie would re-join Sheffield United in a community role and in 1996 he featured beside Sean Bean and Emily Lloyd in the football film *When Saturday Comes*.

While researching this story I managed to jog the memory of legendary Shrimpers striker Roy McDonough for his recollection of Currie's all to brief stay at Roots Hall.

"In training, Peter Morris let him do what he liked," he told me. "We were all doing laps of the pitch whilst Tony was doing keepy-ups with the ball on his own".

Roy also remembered that fateful afternoon against Wimbledon. "Tony walked on the pitch to warm up before the game and I knocked him a ball he chipped it 30 yards back to me and pulled his calf. Off he went back down the tunnel not to be seen again till we found him in the bar where he was sloshed on scotch, he was a great lad though".

In July 2011, some 28-years after Tony's short-lived stay on the Essex Riviera, his nephew, Darren Currie arrived at Roots Hall as the club embarked upon its pre-season schedule. The player with more clubs than Jack Nicklaus had been

Southend United 1983/84. Tony Currie pictured third from the left in the back row.

linked with a move to Southend in the past. Currie junior played bit-part roles in friendly matches at Great Wakering Rovers, Braintree Town and Needham Market; however, that was as far as it went. He would resurface soon after at Blue Square South club Boreham Wood before moving on to Hendon then back into the Football League with Dagenham & Redbridge.

AN AFTERNOON WITH BILLY JENNINGS

In the most unlikely of surroundings, Brian caught up with a former Orient and West Ham star who had an eye for goal.

PRE-SEASON mixes a whole host of footballing cocktails and often sees great players turning up at some unlikely places. This season, Orient v New York Cosmos and Bournemouth v Real Madrid particularly caught my imagination, taking me back to the magical matches I would play out on my Subbuteo as a kid. Therefore, today it seems somewhat symbolic that here I am at Burroughs Park, home of Essex Senior Leaguers Great Wakering Rovers, talking to a former First Division striker while the villagers take on League 2 neighbours Southend United.

Billy Jennings now works as a football agent but he still remembers with some fondness his time in the professional game. During a 12-year career, Jennings amassed 261 Football League appearances for Watford, West Ham, Orient and Luton Town, finding the onion bag an impressive 89 times along the way.

"As a youngster I played football whenever I could," Billy says. This didn't leave him with too many opportunities to watch games, although his father would occasionally take him to see Spurs. Jennings' first opportunity in the professional game came with Watford. "I went there as a kid, learning a lot from the senior players," he exclaims. His first team debut came in unusual surroundings. Back then there used to be a 3rd and 4th place play-off in the FA Cup. Having been knocked out in the semi-final, Watford would face Manchester United at Arsenal's old home, Highbury. "United won 2-0, but facing all their big stars gave me the appetite to nail down a regular place in the team," he says. During a four-year stint at Vicarage Road, Jennings plundered 33 goals in 93 games, something which hadn't gone unnoticed. West Ham United were looking to bolster their attacking options and saw the Hornets youngster as the perfect fit. In August 1974, the Hammers paid £110,000 to secure his services.

"The first time I went to Upton Park was the day I signed for the club," Billy tells me. Nevertheless, he soon made an impact in his new surroundings, scoring on his debut although visitors Sheffield United would snatch victory by the odd goal in three. The elevation in class wasn't lost on Jennings. "I'd gone from the Third Division to the First in the space of a week, with all due respect to Watford it was a real eye opener how different the gulf in standard was at West Ham," he tells me.

While at West Ham, Jennings established himself as a regular goal scorer in the top flight and appeared in several showpiece games along the way. Undoubtedly, the highlight was the 1975 FA Cup Final. At Wembley, West Ham would face a Fulham side that included the legendary Bobby Moore. He remembers that the week leading up to the match was quite intense, but come the day everything passed by very quickly. West Ham won 2-0, but it was far from a classic, Billy recalls. "I seem to remember more about the open top bus parade the following day," he says. "It was a special occasion and seemed like the whole of the East End had come out to see the cup and welcome the team home."

Jennings told me of a whole host of wonderful footballers he played alongside at West Ham, however, two stood out. "Trevor Brooking was a joy to work with; he pulled the strings and made things happen for the forwards." As well as benefiting enormously from Brooking, he is quick to praise the role of skipper Billy Bonds. "Billy had lots of character and was inspirational." He is also keen to point out that both players had earned their status as legends at Upton Park.

A passage of Billy's career not so well documented was a three-month spell in the North American Soccer League, and a chance to rub shoulders with some of the game's biggest stars.

It was at the end of the 1976/77 season. Soccer was largely an alien sport to the American people. Players were shipped in from all over the world in an attempt to give the game's profile a lift. Billy joined Chicago Sting on a three-month loan from West Ham. It was an arrangement that suited both parties – the NASL clubs were keen to get First Division footballers over, it also gave English clubs an opportunity to get a player off the payroll for a short while. Although the standard was not as high as that in England, Billy believed an opportunity to see America was too good to turn down, and he soon settled in. "I didn't know much about the League," he confesses, and that included the fact most clubs played on AstroTurf as opposed to grass.

Billy linked up with an outfit that included a number of English players. Ronnie Moore was over from Rotherham and Willie Morgan from Manchester United. Together they made up a decent front line that plundered 17 goals between them, this all under the guidance of Bill Foulke. "Foulke was a typical old school gaffer," Jennings tells me. "He was a former Busby Babe, and had survived the devastating Munich air crash, he was an interesting man, very straight talking," he adds.

Jennings recalls with a smile the moment he and Morgan first set foot in Chicago.

"I flew over with Willie. Sting had already played four games, lost the lot and were bottom of the league. I guess Bill Foulke got in touch with our respective clubs and asked us to come over as soon as the English league season was over. Part of our deal was accommodation and a car. Willie and I were looking forward to receiving a big American motor each, or so we thought. On arrival, we were presented with a small Datsun each. As you can imagine we were somewhat disappointed, which we voiced to Foulke. He told us he couldn't do anything because they had lost four games and he was under pressure."

Playing in the States also gave Jennings the opportunity to play against some wonderful footballers including George Best, but it was an incident during a game with New York Cosmos that particularly stood out. He explains, "Twenty-one players trotted out on to the pitch, but then we had to wait for Pelé to make a glitzy appearance. We stood there for about ten minutes while he lapped the pitch, the crowd went crazy."

After all the razzmatazz surrounding the Brazilian legend had died down, the match got underway. "I received the ball and turned into one of the Cosmos players, we were both committed but I managed to flick the ball through his legs and wriggle away." Caught up in the flow of the match, Billy hadn't realised that he had just nutmegged Pelé. I shouldn't imagine too many players have that particular claim to fame, in fact I told him had it been me I'd have taken my boots off and retired with immediate effect, how could it have got any better?

Jennings played only one season in the NASL with Chicago Sting. "I wasn't tempted to go back, besides which the opportunity never arose," he tells me.

Of course, since the seventies, football has changed drastically in America. The old NASL folded in 1984; it wasn't until 1996 with the formation of the MLS (Major League Soccer) that a top class competitive form of the game returned. The new league has proved to be extremely popular with the American people, something that surprises Jennings. "We would only get around 4000 turn up at for home games in Chicago," he says. "As you can imagine the crowd would look sparse as we played at the huge Wrigley Field, home of the Chicago Cubs baseball team."

Despite soccer's resurgence, and indeed the fact that it's becoming one of the fastest growing sport across the pond, Bill doesn't see the USA winning the World Cup in the near future, "At the moment, the standard of the league needs to improve and produce more home grown talent, that's not to say they'll never win it though," he explains.

Once back in England, a snapped Achilles interrupted Jennings' Upton Park career. During a lengthy spell on the sidelines, he could only look on as David Cross and Bryan 'Pop' Robson were brought in and West Ham were relegated. Once fit again, he had to be content with a substitute's role. "I was feeling a bit sorry for myself and a bit disillusioned," he says. Billy heard of Orient's interest and so after 99 league games and 34 goals for the Hammers, it was off to Brisbane Road. "I didn't know too much about the O's," he confesses. "Manager Jimmy Bloomfield made me feel wanted, besides I knew Mervyn Day and Tommy Taylor from my time at West Ham."

Although Billy didn't enjoy as much in the way of honours at Orient, he was once again able to perform alongside some excellent footballers. One particular player stood head and shoulders above the rest: "Stan Bowles was a genius, possibly the most technical footballer I've ever seen," he tells me. "Had Stan been a slightly better athlete, and not had his well-documented problems, he could have been the best player this country has ever produced, the fans adored him." At this point, this fledgling interviewer has to move things along. Both of us had great memories of watching Stan play, Billy had some terrific tales of him too. I believe we could have talked about him all afternoon and indeed most of the night given the chance. Finally, though, we moved on. Jennings was a popular figure with the Brisbane Road crowd and proved to be quite productive in front of goal, finding the net 21 times in 67 games between 1979 and 1982.

From Orient, he teamed up with Luton Town who were under the guidance of David Pleat. "I hadn't really got over the injury from my West Ham days; I had lost my sharpness and went to Kenilworth Road simply to muck in from the bench." Billy knew this would be his last season in the professional game. Although he only appeared from the dugout twice, he still managed to stick one in the onion bag and thus kept up his impressive ration of a goal in slightly less than every three Football League games, playing a small part in the Hatters' march to the Second Division title.

After several seasons out of football, Billy was tempted to pull on the boots again. "I missed playing and the dressing room banter, and thought I could still do it," he explains. However, it was a decision he was to regret. The level of expectation directed at him was not matched by his own fitness. After short stints with Dagenham, Bishops Stortford and Heybridge Swifts, he called time on playing once and for all.

These days, Bill loves his job as a player's agent, and tells me, "It gives me the chance to go and watch plenty of games." Personally, I'm delighted that someone from the generation I'd label 'real footballers' still has a healthy appetite for the beautiful game. Of course, the multi-millionaire players who today grace the highest echelons of the English game probably won't have to look for an alternative career once their boots are hung up. I for one wonder if they will ever have any tales worth passing on to those who once idolised them, or for that matter if they'll ever experience the delights of watching football at Great Wakering!

STUBBS AND FRENCH HIT FORM FOR ENGLAND

W ITH THE HELSINKI GAMES of 1952 rapidly approaching, Walter Winterbottom, joint manager of the England and Great Britain football teams, looked to put his charges to the test before the qualifying matches for the Olympics.

On 30th April 1952, Winterbottom saw an opportunity not only to give his Olympians some match practice but also to run the rule over some of the countries up and coming talent by pitching them against an England B team at Highbury Stadium, home of Arsenal Football Club.

Lined up to play for the England team were several bright prospects such as Brentford's Ron Greenwood (a future West Ham United and England manager), Tottenham Hotspur's Bobby Smith, and Jimmy Hill of Fulham. The match attracted a great deal of local interest when Southend United's Great-Wakering-born Outside Left, Les Stubbs, and Right Half John 'Jackie' French, a native of Stockton and formerly of Middlesbrough who'd joined the Shrimpers in 1947 after finishing his national service with the 121 Training Regiment, Royal Artillery, were also included.

The plucky Olympians, all amateur players, proved to be no match for the young Lions, who ran out winners by three goals to nil, with both Stubbs and French finding the net. Tommy Harmer of Tottenham Hotspur grabbed the other England goal. Interestingly, Bill Healey played for England in the second half having already played for Arsenal in a London Combination Cup fixture that afternoon, what's more, the game went to extra time!

The Southend Pictorial, dated 2nd May 1952, ran the headline 'FRENCH AND STUBBS SHONE FOR ENGLAND B.'

It went on to say how Leslie Stubbs had opened the scoring in the 12th minute, with Jackie French scoring midway through the second half.

The *Pictorial* described French as being one of the best players on the pitch and that he gave a "grand performance as an attacking wing-half."

The Great Britain team would continue their preparations with a couple of matches against Germany, losing 2-1 in Dusseldorf, then 2-0 in Nürnberg.

They fared little better at the XV Olympiad in Finland. After being humiliated 5-3 by Luxembourg in Lahti, Great Britain would then lose 4-2 at the hands of Greece in Hämeenlinna. Having embarrassingly been eliminated before the opening ceremony, most of the British players stayed in Finland to play several hastily arranged friendly matches against local sides in order to recoup some of the losses incurred by the FA following the team's early exit.

Later that year the beleaguered Great Britain team finally ended their run of defeats after recovering from two goals down to claim a creditable 2-2 draw with Norway in Oslo.

Jackie French would go on to play 198 games for Southend scoring 22 goals either side of an injury-hit spell with Nottingham Forest. Towards the end of his career, he played for Folkestone Town before becoming the manager of Basildon United. Despite his North Eastern roots, his heart was clearly in South East Essex. He would return to Southend United to work for the supporters club.

As for Les Stubbs, his 83 appearances and 40 goals for Southend, including 14 goals in 14 games at the start of the 52/53 season, enticed Chelsea to shell out £10,000 for his services. During almost six years at Stamford Bridge Stubbs scored 35 goals in 123 appearances. He would win a First Division champions medal (1954/55) followed by a Charity Shield winners gong (Chelsea beating Newcastle 3-0). He would also represent London in the Inter-City Fairs Cup before returning to Southend United for two seasons in 1958. Stubbs played a season at Southern League Bedford Town before returning home to join Great Wakering Rovers.

At Rovers he would capture the imagination of the locals who packed the Wakering Rec touchlines to get a glimpse of the 'local boy who'd done good'. He would be a pivotal part of a team that dominated the Southend & District League for more than a decade.

Featured pictures include extracts from the four-page match programme, available on the day for 3d, but today selling at £50, as well as Stubbs' match itinerary sent by the Football Association. It states that players and officials should make their own travel arrangements. All the footballers would be paid travel expenses and the 'professionals' a match fee of £6. Unlike the pampered stars of today, the players were requested to bring with them soap and towels!

SOUTHEND'S
SCINTILLATING
SHOOTING
SPECIALIST

GREAT WAKERING GET THE WORLD CUP WILLIE'S

Brian on duty for Football.com at Burroughs Park

Great Wakering Rovers 0-4 Canvey Island

IT'S FORTY-SEVEN YEARS to the day since the English game celebrated its finest achievement, winning the World Cup. Since that memorable Wembley triumph over West Germany, the country's footballing masses have been treated to an accumulation of disappointments, penalty heartache and generally feeling sorry for themselves, with the occasional 'nearly' thrown in for good measure. So, what to do to commemorate this aging landmark? Simple, visit the Doomsday Village and spend the night reminiscing, whilst taking in a friendly fixture between two of the games great footballing outposts, Great Wakering Rovers and Canvey Island.

At this point, I sense a few raised eyebrows. However, for those of us in the Burroughs Park press box, this game, like every other we watch, is every bit as special. My faithful sidekick Ed, and Glen Eckett, who is scribing for the Islanders programme and website, join me in the 'special seats'. Not only that, but sitting just along from us is a bloke who looks uncannily like Bobby Charlton, it couldn't be... could it?

Nonetheless, why a legendary Manchester United and England player would visit us doomsdayers is anyone's guess. Perhaps, like us, he needed something to take his mind of the years of hurt that have followed his and indeed our, finest hour... unlikely, but hey, we're at a football match, taking in its spontaneous urban flow, and that as far as we are concerned, is living the dream.

Anyway, game on. Rovers create the opening opportunity, but Dan Trenkel's cross is headed clear by Rob Bartley, though it is clear that Canvey have settled the quicker. After Rovers defender Nathan Fletcher cut out Jay Curran's searching cross, the Gulls grabbed the lead. From the resulting flag kick, Rio Bryan-Edwards soared above the throng within the box to power a header past goalkeeper Adam Seal and high into the net.

Pictured in the Rovers press box with Glen Eckett.

Canvey are now under the management of former player Danny Heale, an instantly likeable chap who is determined to do things his way. During a loan spell at Burroughs Park during the previous campaign, it was clear to see he was a thinking man's footballer. Now, given the chance to pass all that knowledge on, his charges respond with some crisp neat football that is quite pleasant on the eye. After Seal had denied Curran with a quite brilliant save, the visitors doubled their advantage. Seal did well to keep out Simon Thomas' effort, only for Spencer Bellotti to fire home from close range.

Rovers looked for a way back. Nick Humphrey cleared his lines as Trenkel lurked at the far post, while Jay Smith should perhaps have done better, heading Gary Paterson's centre wide of the target. Nevertheless, before the home side could make any headway, the deficit increased. Bellotti was enjoying his evening, and just before the half time brew, he raced away before beating Seal with aplomb to put the outcome beyond doubt.

One would have expected Rovers to return to the fray with a flea in their ear, however, the Islanders started where they left off. Seal flew out to hack clear from the on-rushing Thomas, and then the Great Wakering custodian sprung to his right, turning aside Matt Games long-range strike.

The home side's sporadic attacks bore little fruit. Joe Skeels half chance was snubbed out by the Canvey rearguard while Paterson's ball across the goal found no takers after the Rovers front man had done well to round Dale Brightly.

After Thomas had scuffed a glorious opportunity, Canvey eventually made it four-nil. Seal misjudged the bounce of the ball and the ever-alert Bellotti was on hand to make the most of the keepers blunder. What's this, a hat trick, forty-seven years to the day! Perhaps it's a sign? I wondered what our Bobby Charlton look-alike was thinking… unless… no it couldn't be… could it?

Whistler Steve Parmenter expertly dealt with a bout of over exuberance late in the day. I like 'Parms' style of refereeing; he played the game at a decent level with Bristol Rovers and was capped by Wales at Under 21 level. Note to the Football Association, former players know the game better than some of the numb nuts we supporters have to endure week in week out, up and down the county. Another pointer to the FA's bigwigs is that in business (you keep reminding us football is a business), the customer is always right, something they seem to have conveniently forgotten.

With the game in its burning embers, Bobby Charlton makes his exit. "He thinks it's all over" Ed cries out, and regardless of Bellotti missing a late chance, the shriek of Parmenter's whistle confirms, that it is now.

Great Wakering Rovers: Seal, Radley, Read, Benjamin, Hepburn, Fletcher, Skeels, Trenkel, Paterson, Williams, Smith.

Great Wakering Rovers substitutes: Matt Hambleton, Harry Skinner, Malaki Toussaint, Tom Roberts, Louis Godwin – Green.

Canvey Island: Brightly, Sellears, Humphrey, Game, Bartley, Bryan-Edwards, Curran, Nash, Thomas, Bellotti, Dumas.

Canvey Island substitutes: Sands, Baucutt, Alaile.

ROD HULL – A FOOTBALLING TRAGEDY

On March 17th 1999, the entertainer Rod Hull was accidently killed in what could be described as a tragic football related accident.

RODNEY STEPHEN HULL was born in the Isle of Sheppey on August 13th 1935. Hull made fame and fortune with his sidekick, Emu, a vicious hand puppet who notoriously savaged a clutch of celebrities including Johnny Carson and Richard Pryor. Emu's most famous victim was chat show host Michael Parkinson. The attack proved one of the most iconic British television moments of the seventies, and prompted another guest on the show, comedian, musician and Celtic fan Billy Connelly, to warn Hull, "If that bird comes anywhere near me, I'll break its neck and your bloody arm!"

Despite his Kentish origins, Rod Hull for some reason supported Bristol Rovers. His dedication to 'The Gas' proven when he wrote, and sung (with Emu) the 1974 track "I'm Singing Bristol Rovers all the way" (to the tune of "She'll be coming 'round the mountain").

Some folk have described the tune as "the worst football song of all time," although I have to say my kids seem to like it!

On that fateful March night, 63-year-old Hull had been watching the Champions League match between Inter Milan and Manchester United on television at his home in Winchelsea, East Sussex where he lived with his son Oliver.

The TV picture became distorted so Hull attempted to scale the roof of his house to adjust the aerial.

Some reports suggest that the entertainer climbed up wearing his house slippers, which would have proved to be hopelessly inadequate on the slippery rooftop. Others, that he may have suffered a heart attack, either whilst climbing or after the accident.

What is clear is that Hull fell from the roof and through a greenhouse, causing a severe skull fracture and chest injuries. Oliver said he heard a light thud followed by a heavy thud. He found his father lying on the floor and called for help. Hull senior was pronounced dead on arrival in hospital in nearby Hastings. The coroner later reported a verdict of accidental death.

The pathologist examining the entertainer's body found that his judgement might well have been impaired by alcohol. Nevertheless, he added it was not a level that would be in any way incapacitating.

* * *

For the record, Paul Scholes 88th minute goal for Manchester United cancelled out Ventola's strike for the Italian's midway through the second half. United would go on to lift the trophy for the first time since 1968, defeating Bayern Munich 2-1 in a dramatic final in Barcelona.

* * *

"I'm singing Bristol Rovers all the way," never caught on as the clubs anthem. Instead, you'll find 'Gasheads' singing, "Goodnight Irene," which is thought to have originated from a big victory over Plymouth Argyle in the 1950's, with the words, "Goodnight Argyle," being directed at visiting Devonians who'd had enough and were leaving the old Eastville ground early.

As for Emu, he and another of Hull's sons, Toby, formed a partnership, firstly in pantomime then in 2007 with their own television show.

THE BUCKET AND SPADE BRIGADE!

Brian, 'Shouting from the rooftops at Southchurch Park Arena'

Southend Manor 4-0 Eton Manor

"OH I DO LIKE to be beside the seaside"... and today that 'like' is somewhere close to where the angry North Sea meets the all-together more tranquil waves of the Thames. Mid table Southend Manor's weather hit Essex Senior League campaign, reaches it's conclusion with equally cosy Eton Manor the visitors to Southchurch Park Arena.

The finale has come too soon for the Seasider's; they have found a bit of form lately and are playing with some panache. Eton Manor have been equally frustrating this term, beating promotion hopefuls Barkingside and Takeley but then stumbling against lowly Bowers & Pitsea and Stansted.

Nevertheless, the mindset of the non-league footballer is somewhat different to that of the Premiership stars. If you have spent all week working in an office or on a factory floor waiting for 3pm Saturday, then there is no way you're going to pass up an opportunity to let off steam with a few full blooded tackles and an over powering sense of devotion. The chance to be today's 'Lord of the Manor's' will ensure both side do everything in their power to make that post match pint taste extra sweet.

Southchurch Park might not attract too much attention these days, but the ground does embrace a rich piece of local sporting history. On 15th May 1948,

Southchurch Park Arena.

Sir Donald Bradman and the all-conquering Australian cricket team smashed 721 here in their tour match with Essex. The huge total is still a world record for runs scored in a single day, and the thumping innings and 451 run thumping is still the county's heaviest defeat. More than 16,000 spectators crammed into the park that day, sixty-five years later the crowd is somewhat less significant, but nonetheless, a turnout of 91 is quite respectable for the ESL.

The Arena stand is somewhat ugly. It is awash with unusual graffiti, has a number of vandalised seats and offers a smell you expect from a tower block lift! Not a pretty image I know, but as the wind howls and storm clouds gather, it offers its dwellers some solace from the elements.

The audience has been bolstered by a late surge at the turnstile. A number of Southend United and Great Wakering Rovers supporters have filed in. Clearly, they still have the football bug, despite a disappointing conclusion to their respective seasons.

My good friend Gerry Smith from Phoenix FM joins me in the stand. Gerry should be at Wembley today watching the FA Vase Final. However, the tickets, and the neighbour I left them with (who we'll refer to as Mr X), have gone mysteriously missing. It turns out Mr X has just returned following a short holiday at Her Majesty's pleasure, one suspects he's up to his old trick and has helped himself to a free day out using my beleaguered buddies tickets.

Southend Manor are quickest out of the traps. Aldaberto Pinto's free kick falls to Terry Griffiths, but a combination of Joe Kizzi and keeper Carl Young snub out the danger. Then Pinto produces a piece of magic. A cross between Maradona and Robin Cousins, pirouetting majestically with the ball seemingly glued to his foot. This crystallised flash of brilliance lead up a blind alleyway, but the spectators appreciate the moment all the same.

It is not long before the home side break the deadlock. Gary Paterson display's predator instincts, turning and then beating Young with a crisp finish.

Eton Manor search for an immediate route back. Southend custodian Adam Seal expertly flips John Bricknell's dead ball effort over the top, and then the busy Darryl Wilson beats the keeper with a lob, but can only look on as his enterprising attempt falls wide of the target.

The blustery wet conditions and bumpy surface make it difficult to produce any kind of expansive football; this becomes even trickier when the cloudburst turns into a fully blown thunderstorm. However, to their credit, the players attempt to play a passing game as opposed to the long ball that so many people associate with this echelon of the game.

The visitor's quest for parity is thwarted when Brad Vaughan produces a wonderful saving tackle on Wilson. At the other end the Seasider's go close with both Paterson and Vaughan narrowly off target.

Then like a lightning bolt to match that from the heavens, goal scorer Paterson appears a little late on Josh Sykes, sparking a bout of 'handbags' amongst the players. Once the mêlée had subsided, Pato is brandished a red card by whistler Mr Stanley, while Sykes leaves the field via a stretcher. It is a sad conclusion to the season for Paterson. He is clearly not 'that type of player', whether his actions were a rush of blood or simply mistimed, he is clearly upset with himself as he leaves the field. Thankfully, the Eton Manor players' injury is not as bad as is first feared.

However, any thoughts that the ten men would buckle are soon dispersed. Yaw Danso sends a wonderful curling effort beyond the extended Young to double the home sides' advantage.

Eton Manor use the interval to regroup, they emerge for the second period and carve out the first chance. Danny Walsh makes an impressive dash down the right flank but his teasing centre eludes an influx of possible takers. John Bricknell is next to try his luck, forcing Seal into a smart save from his free kick, then the big stopper earns his corn, denying Wilson low to his left.

Nevertheless, any lingering hopes of a comeback was scuppered when the impressive Mark Sission latched onto Danso's pass before dispatching the ball home through the legs of Young. Sission is clearly an asset to the Southchurch Park club. He capped an excellent personal and team performance by racing clear then finishing with aplomb to make it 4-0.

In the burning embers, the game becomes a little flat. What with the contest now over, Gerry's attention turns from the football to politics and then the distressing break-up of JLS, he believes that our combination of boyish good looks and a nice light baritone could provide us with an opportunity to fill the void they have created. Personally, I question who provides which, if either, and wonder if Mr X is having such an afternoon of intellect at the home of football. Meanwhile, Eton Manor's Gary Wright makes a late attempt to recapture our attention with a snap shot at the home sides goal, however, his effort, much like the conversation, was wayward.

Southend Manor: Seal, Jarrett, East, Griffiths, Vaughan, Pinto, Danso, Pibworth, Paterson, Sisson, Smith.

Substitutes: Jude, Baldwin, Welsh, Ivie, Salmon.

Eton Manor: Young, Heywood, Wright, Johnson, Sykes, Kizzi, Bradbury, J Giddings, Wilson, Bricknell, Walsh.

Substitutes: Scott, L Giddings, Wallace.

Attendance: 91.

MILLION POUND MADNESS!

In February 1979, the footballing world, according to my Dad, went stark-raving bloody mad!

B IRMINGHAM CITY'S exciting striker Trevor Francis had been attracting a fair bit of attention following a string of eye-catching performances and a clutch of goals. With the Blues struggling to make any real headway in the First Division, it was clear that his future lies away from St Andrews and it was no surprise when Brian Clough's League Champions, Nottingham Forest, came calling. However, when a transfer fee of £1,000,000 was set, and indeed met, a cool £500,000 more than the previous record (David Mills move from Middlesbrough to West Bromwich Albion just a month before hand), the football world and my Dad went doolally!

One million pounds (1.18 million to be exact) was a lot of money in 1979, as indeed it is today. After all, you wouldn't catch me turning my nose up at it! Nevertheless, in football terms this was deemed ludicrous, how on earth could a footballer be worth so much? In reality, Francis' fee was £999,999 as gaffer Clough didn't want to burden his new recruit with the label 'first million pound footballer'. However, with tax and various 'add-ons' the amount passed seven figures by almost £200,000 and Francis' place in the history and record book was secured.

Francis was famously introduced to the media by a manager impatient to play a game of squash. Clough was clad in a red gym kit and carrying a racquet as he spoke to the nation's press.

The national press had a field day, jumping on the story from the outset. Everyone had an opinion, some suggesting this would be the gateway to a

Brian pictured with Trevor Francis.

never ending spree of big money moves (which of course it was). Others, like my old man, were disgusted by the shear financial vulgarity, believing this would be the first and last time such a sum would be exchanged for a British professional footballer. "You'll never see a transfer like that again" Dad scoffed heatedly as he peered over the sports pages of the newspaper at me.

Of course, for those of us still in short trousers, Trevor Francis' move had an effect on trading in the school yard. Forest's sensational signing was now a sort after commodity. His bubble-gum card and Panini sticker was now worth three of any other. Some kids argued that if Francis was worth three, how many cards would you need to swap for a Kenny Dalglish, Stan Bowles or Liam Brady?

Trevor Francis' Nottingham Forest career was perhaps deemed a little disappointing considering the magnitude of his arrival. However, he made 70 appearances for the club, scoring 28 goals. Unquestionably, his 'cigar moment' for the East Midlands outfit would forever be etched in the memories of Forest supporters. In Munich on May 30th 1979 against Swedish Champions Malmo

FF, he stooped to head home John Robertson's left wing cross for the only goal, thus ensuring Forest their first European Cup success and almost certainly compensating for a large slice of that record fee.

Meanwhile, in Manchester, the Blues half of the City were expecting big things. Manchester City chairman Peter Swales and his flamboyant manager Malcolm Allison had brought in several high-profile players, forking out a tidy sum in the process. But as yet, the spending extravaganza had yielded little success on the pitch. Their latest target in a bid to spearhead a dash for silverware was Wolverhampton Wanderers talented midfielder Steve Daley. City were keen to get their man as well as spinning the media spotlight upon themselves, and so in September 1979 they smashed the Francis deal, landing Daley for a staggering £1,437,500.

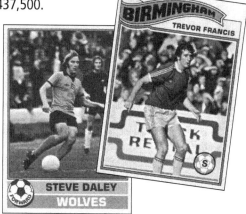

But it soon became clear that Daley and Manchester City were far from a perfect match. Saddled by expectation and the huge fee, Daley endured a miserable time at Maine Road, making 48 appearances, scoring just 4 goals. Branded, "The biggest waste of money in football history," Daley's stay in Manchester ended in 1981 when he was allowed to join North American League club Seattle Sounders for a knock-down fee of £300,000.

Malcolm Allison would soon find himself out on his arse. Together he and Swales bickered over Daley's transfer, both claiming the other had inflated the fee.

As for Francis. He would leave Forest in 1981, ironically joining Manchester City for another fee in excess of a million quid. He would later play for Rangers, Sheffield Wednesday, Queen's Park Rangers as well as Italian clubs Sampdoria and Atalanta.

After managing former clubs Birmingham, Wednesday, QPR along with a spell at Crystal Palace, Francis would turn to punditry.

Steve Daley would return to England in 1983 with Burnley before briefly joining Walsall. I fondly remember standing on the Hillary Street End at Fellows Park, watching him play a part in Alan Buckley's attack minded team of the mid-eighties. Opposing fans would often somewhat cruelly remind him of his disastrous spell at City, chanting "What a waste of money". He later turned out as an after dinner speaker, reciting tales of his dark days at Maine Road.

If the events of 1979 had my old man shaking his head in disbelief, then the transfers of both Cristiano Ronaldo (£80m) and Gareth Bale (£85.3m) to Real Madrid from Manchester United and Tottenham Hotspur would have had him turning in his grave!

And to top that off, having watched the likes of Clapton, Leytonstone and Walthamstow Avenue when the players earned barely enough to cover their half-time cuppa, Dad would have had a fit when on 17th May 2012, striker Jamie Vardy, then of Conference Premier Champions Fleetwood Town, became the World's first one million pound non-league player, joining Leicester City.

Several weeks before this book was published I was lucky enough to meet orchestrator Trevor Francis when I was reporting on a Premier League game at West Ham United. He laughed when I told him of Dad's reaction to his record breaking transfer. He went on to tell me, "I didn't feel any pressure as I knew it wouldn't be too long before the record was broken."

But as we ominously close in on the world's first £100 million footballer, one has to ask – "Where will the madness end?"

GAMES WITHOUT FRONTIERS

Leyton Orient 2-1 New York Cosmos

A S LEYTON ORIENT and New York Cosmos line up on the Brisbane Road greenery, my mind casts back to my squandered adolescence. The pitch crudely placed on our dining table with floodlights adorning each corner. O's were sporting their famous braces kit (without doubt, the best football strip of all time) and were a man light after our cat had pounced upon Bill Roffey, causing the defender a double leg break. Despite the intervention of superglue, the injury had never properly healed thus leaving Orient at a permanent disadvantage. Cosmos wore a green, yellow and white number… actually, it was Tampa Bay Rowdies but the colours were close enough, although I did have trouble pretending Rodney Marsh was now Pelé. Anyway, I didn't think the bumper crowd that consisted of my Mum (who was peeling spuds) and Dad (reading the paper), would give two hoots. This of course was Subbuteo, anything goes, and anyone can play each other, but surely, this particular match up could never happen?

Nonetheless, I should have known better. Orient has history in the art of imaginative exhibition matches as games against the international teams of Wales and Sierra Leone demonstrate. Two of football's more iconic names are going head-to-head, and this time it's for real!

It might be difficult for an O's fan to comprehend how a follower of chief rivals Southend United can feel at home here at Brisbane Road, but reminiscences of a long lost childhood can be special. I glance down from the media area at the Buckingham Road end of the ground. It was where I stood when Dad first brought me here to see Second Division football all those years ago. The place has changed a great deal since we watched the likes of Laurie Cunningham, Tony Grealish and Ian Moores, for me it has lost some of its character. Another poignant thought is that along with Dad, these legends of my infancy are now plying their trade at that big stadium in the sky, an indication that life, just like football, does not stand still forever.

The Cosmos are back in business after an absence of 27 years. The remarketed brainchild of former Tottenham Hotspur vice-chairman Paul Kemsley and supported by former player Pelé. Of course, these days they can't boast the talent of the Brazilian legend, nor for that matter Franz Beckenbauer or Carlos Alberto who starred alongside him during the heydays of the 1970s. However, they do possess the notable talent of Marcos Senna, who graced La Liga for eleven years with Villarreal and gained 28 international caps for Spain.

Orient make a bright start. Cosmos goalkeeper Jimmy Maurer is forced to hack clear as David Mooney lurks, then Kevin Lisbie heads over following Lloyd James' pinpoint free kick.

Cosmos slowly find their feet. Former MK Dons and Southend United man, Jemal Johnson fizzes a hat-trick of chances outside the frame of the goal without troubling Os' keeper Jamie Jones too much.

Lisbie is looking sharp; first he sends another headed effort over, and soon after his trickery has Cosmos in a spin. Unfortunately, his cross can't match the fancy footwork as it eludes all comers and drops harmlessly wide.

The teams continue to exchange blows. Johnson has Jones scrambling across his goal, while Maurer awkwardly fists clear another James free kick, drawing a chorus of "dodgy keeper" from the Brisbane Road faithful.

Nevertheless, Orient have clearly settled the better, and after twenty-three minutes, they are in front. The Cosmos have survived a clutch of dangerous corners from James. However, when the visitors fail to clear yet another of his flag kicks, David Mooney pounces to fire in despite the desperate attempts of the beleaguered American rearguard.

The Cosmos hit back instantly. Ayoze's turn and ferocious strike is brilliantly turned over by Jones, while during the melée from a flag kick, quite astonishingly, both Joseph Nane and Alessandro Noselli hit the Os' woodwork. In between, Maurer blocks from Moses Odubajo with his feet after Lisbie has picked him out with a quite exquisite pass.

Just after the half time cuppa, the game has a somewhat lacklustre feel to it. The play is untidy and frustrating as passes go astray and tackles are untimely. Eventually, after some ten minutes of getting it out of their system, Orient create an opening. Lisbie finds strike partner Mooney but Maurer saves his snap shot smartly.

As the game approaches the hour mark, the home side double their advantage. Noselli appears to hold Mathieu Baudry and whistler Stuart Attwell has no hesitation in pointing to the penalty spot. Lisbie dispatches the kick low to his left, sending Maurer the wrong way in the process.

Orient have the bit between their teeth. Maurer produces a brilliant save from James' curling free kick as the Londoners threaten to pull clear, while in response, Senna of the Cosmos sees his tame place kick expertly fielded by Jones. However, with a quarter of an hour remaining, Cosmos are handed an unlikely lifeline. O's custodian Jones has been a largely redundant figure during the second period, but when faced with his first meaningful task of the evening, he can only glance back in anguish as Sebastian Guenzatti's speculative attempt slips through his hands and into the net. The goal gives the visitors renewed vigour. Ayoze sees his free kick scrambled clear while Noselli heads a golden opportunity over after Hunter Freeman has galloped down the right flank to deliver.

Cosmos' late rally bears no further fruit, however, Orient hold firm for a deserved victory. Of course, it's difficult to predict the outcome of the season that lies ahead, but on this evidence, the Londoners look in pretty good shape.

The teams embrace and disappear down the tunnel to warm applause from the small but content gathering of 2,004. As yet, there is no talk of a return fixture, however, if anyone's up for it, I'll climb up into the loft and dust off those plastic legends from days gone by. I'd imagine Shoeburyness, Leyton and the Bronx are much the same in the wacky world of Subbuteo.

Leyton Orient: Jamie Jones, Gary Sawyer, Scott Cuthbert (Omozusi – 69), Nathan Clarke, Mathieu Baudry (Vanderhyde – 84); Moses Odubajo, Lloyd James (Lee – 69), Romain Vincelot, Shaun Batt; David Mooney (Adda Djaziri (trialist) 86), Kevin Lisbie (Georgiou – 76).

Leyton Orient substitutes: Jake Larkins (GK), Jack Sheratt, Adda Djaziri.

New York Cosmos: Jimmy Maurer, Hunter Freeman, Hunter Gorskie (Veeder – 69), Carlos Mendes, Joseph Nane; Ayoze, Roversio, Marcos Senna, Diomar Diaz (Lopez – 69), Satoru Kashiwase (Noselli – 36), Jemal Johnson (Guenzatti – 54).

New York Cosmos substitutes: Peri Marosevic, Chad Calderone, Danny Szetela, Dane Murphy, Stefan Dimitrov, Chris Reed, David Diosa, Juan Gonzalez, Kyle Reynish, Hagop Chirishian, Paulo Mendes.

GREAT WAKERING ROVERS 1
LEYTON ORIENT 1

Saturday 18th July 1992 was a landmark day in the history of sleepy
South East Essex village Great Wakering.

Wakering's main claim to fame is that it's mentioned in the Doomsday
Book and sighted as one of the driest places in Britain, but up to now,
the place had never staged a senior football match!

Nevertheless, on that sundrenched afternoon twenty-something summers
ago, all that was about to change. Local club, Great Wakering Rovers had
proved to be a dominant force at Essex Intermediate level. Now after the
clubs Burroughs Park ground was given the Football Association's seal of
approval to stage a high grade of soccer, they found themselves elevated to
the giddy heights of the Essex Senior League where they would rub shoulders
with local football giants such as Concord Rangers, Hullbridge Sports and
Southend Manor.

However, before a ball was to be kicked in anger, the Rovers had an impressive
list of pre-season friendly games lined-up to wet the appetite.

Southend United would be sending a team as would the newly amalgamated
Dagenham & Redbridge who had chosen Great Wakering Rovers as their first
ever opponents under their new guise. But before those mouth watering matches,
the Rovers would play their inaugural fixture as a senior club, with Third Division
Leyton Orient providing the opposition.

The club were keen to share their big day with as many people as possible. In the lead-up to the momentous fixture, respected local newspaper hack, Dick Marshall, gave Great Wakering top billing with a sizable plug in the Echo. Prices were set at £1.50p with the elderly paying a pound and children admitted free.

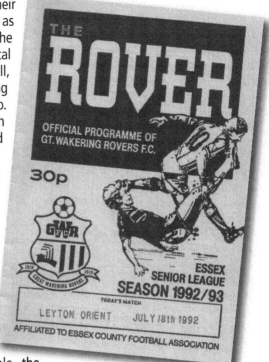

Come the big day a crowd of around the five-hundred mark descended upon Burroughs Park, including a good contingent from Orient and a fair few curious ground hoppers. Match programmes sold out in double quick time with some collectors so determined not to miss out, they would offer those in possession more than double the thirty-pence cover price to acquire the treasured souvenir.

For the record, Great Wakering acquitted themselves well against a young but keen Leyton Orient side managed by former West Ham United midfielder Geoff Pike. It took until the seventy-first minute before the Football League side broke the villager's resilience, Paul Cobb the Londoners goal scorer.

However, this was Great Wakering's day. Two minutes later, referee Gordon Chittock pointed to the penalty spot and Martin Tyrell made no mistake levelling the score and giving the Rovers a share of the spoils.

At the final whistle, I departed the ground, stopping briefly at the Exhibition Pub to 'medicinally' collect my thoughts assisted with a pint of Best Bitter, before catching the bus home to Rochford via Shoeburyness.

I was pleased to have another senior football venue to catch a match, even if it was a little awkward to get too. Little did I realise within a few years I'd be moving four miles east and Great Wakering Rovers would become my local club. Visits to Burroughs Park would become commonplace, friendships with some wonderfully colourful characters were forged. Another rollercoaster had been boarded and despite being something of a footballing backwater compared to the hustle and bustle of the Premiership, The Rovers and its people had become an important part of my life.

Soccer's back as Wakering host O's

By DICK MARSHALL

IT may only be a few short weeks since Denmark won the European Championship, but soccer's already back on the sporting scene.

Tomorrow sees the start of the pre-season friendly programme with a particularly attractive fixture at Burroughs Park, Wakering, when Great Wakering Rovers, about to embark on their first season as a senior club, take on a Leyton Orient XI.

Rovers, due to kick-off for the first time in the Essex Senior League in just over a month, are likely to rely mainly on the men who saw them to four trophies last campaign.

One notable absentee tomorrow is seasoned campaigner David Wale who has not as yet committed himself to the Wakering cause for the coming season.

New men in action tomorrow include Billy Herbert, Kim Walker and goalkeeper Lee Ballard, who have all left the Stambridge camp following that side's drop back from senior status to the ranks of intermediate football.

Another current trialist is Mark Cook, formerly with Wakering's Essex Intermediate League rivals Rayleigh Town.

Although tomorrow's Orient side is likely to include only one regular member of the East London side's first team League squad in Paul Cobb, there is likely to be some exciting young talent in the visiting line-up including former Billericay Town and England Schools' defensive star Dominic Ludden.

The Orient party is being brought to Wakering by former West ham and Orient star Geoff Pike.

Entry will be £1.50 tomorrow, £1 for pensioners, but free to children.

Next big game at Wakering is the first ever match for the newly-formed Conference side Dagenham and Redbridge, an amalgamation of the two clubs, who come to Burroughs Park tomorrow week. Southend United are then the visitors on July 29 with a 7.15pm kick-off.

Tomorrow's match, which kicks off at 3pm, is being sponsored by Alan Drewer and Tony Ellison, partners in the Basildon based firm Pyramid Security Systems.

Billericay Town, busily preparing for their first season in the Diadora League First Division, have a low-key start to their friendly build-up tomorrow at Spartan League Cheshunt (2pm).

Their big pre-season home games are Wednesday July 29 (7.30pm) v Leyton Orient followed by a clash with West Ham on Saturday August 1 (3pm).

GERMAN ADVENTURES

Brian celebrates his wife's birthday and grabs a cheeky football fix to boot!

MY WIFE VICTORIA is pretty amazing. She has supported me with endless crazy football projects, and presented me with three soccer mad sons. But, this weekend she has taken it all to a whole new level, twenty-five miles west of Venus in fact!

Vicky has a significant birthday (no, I can't tell you, It's rude to ask a lady her age). She's keen on a weekend away, and despite the attraction of Las Vegas, Barcelona and Gillingham (Yep, we did, don't ask!) She has made my day by announcing she would like to go and see our friends in Germany.

Our destination is the beautiful village of Faid, a stones throw from Cochem on the banks of the river Mosel. I first brought Vicky here shortly after we met. I used to fetch my Sunday league football team here on tour, and have subsequently visited for the World Cup finals and big Bundesliga games. The people of the village are a friendly lot, and I'm pleased to say have always made me and my family welcome. Nevertheless, life changes. Our children came along and our trekking had to be put on ice. In fact, it's been five years since we last visited, I've missed the people, the place, and I simply can't wait to get there.

Ok, now I hear what you're saying. Shouldn't it be Vicky who can't wait to get there, after all it is her birthday? And you'd be right, I have booked her a pampered session at a local health and beauty parlour, a wine tasting and shopping time in Koblenz. It all sounds very pleasant, and indeed it is. But

Koln fans

what's in it for me? Well, while the cat is away, the proverbial mouse will be doing what he does best, seeking out some football!

As ever, we are staying at the Gasthaus Fritzen in Faid. Man of the house is Bernd Pauly, a long-time acquaintance of mine and to my knowledge the biggest supporter of 1 FC Koln on the planet! Vicky's friend Leanne has joined us for the weekend, while the girls are enjoying a full facial and a massage, we'll be off to the big city to take in 1 FC Koln versus VfR Aalen.

1 FC Koln 0-0 VfR Aalen

THE RHEIN ENERGIE STADION is a fantastic place to watch football, in the past I have seen a ferocious derby with Borussia Monchen-gladbach and a Second Round World Cup tie between Ukraine and Switzerland, this afternoon's is a somewhat more low-key affair as 1 FC Koln, now in Bundesliga 2 take on mid table VfR Aalen. Needless to say, with the home side at the top of the table, and a fanatical backing of more than forty-five thousand fans, the game will be deemed every bit as important.

It turned out to be a frustrating afternoon as a well drilled VfR Aalen held out for a goalless draw. It could have been worse for Koln, custodian Timo Horn did well to claw out Joel Pohjanpalo's first half header. The visitors furiously protested believing the goal bound effort had crossed the line, TV picture later proved that their claims were accurate.

Despite the lack of viable goalmouth action, the fans spirits were lifted during the break when Koln mascot, a billy goat by the name of Hennes, slipped his leash and made a dash for the pitch. The crowd roared with delight as the quick-witted creature slipped a number of attempts to re-capture him. In the end, stadium stewards used a pincer movement to outwit the four-legged invader, much to the disappointment of the masses in the stands. Indeed, the following day's newspaper headlined *"Danke Hennes"*! (Thanks Hennes!) It suggested that the unusual pitch invasion was the highlight of the day!

The second period was one-way traffic, with Koln going agonisingly close to grabbing an all-important goal. VfR Aalen keeper Jasmin Fejzic saved from Patrick Helmes with his feet, while substitutes Bard Finne sent two long-range attempts just past an upright. Strangely, I often find it easier to scribe my thought on a game where I have no emotional tie's, but as Bernd winces and groans with every wayward foray, I see a mirror image of myself back home watching Southend United. Proof that whoever you support and wherever you're from, in the great scheme of things, us football fans are very much alike!

Regardless of the result, the fans always make a Koln game a special occasion, their non-stop singing generate one of the best atmosphere's I've ever witnessed. I've always believed that going to a football match is a special gift, and I'm not wanting to open a can of worms about its better elsewhere than back home. However, the stark truth is that this afternoon's attendance was bigger than any on the same day in the Barclays Premier League, pricing was cheaper than our fourth tier and there was a noticeable absence of overzealous policing and stewarding. On top of that, if I so wished I could drink a beer and smoke whilst watching the game, further proof that football fans in Britain are still treated with contempt by the authorities who should be encouraging the growth of the game! We sink a few beers before heading back to Faid. There is no time to dwell for superfan Bernd, his focus is already on Wednesday night's encounter with Karlsrhuer SC!

1 FC Koln: Timo Horn, Miso Brecko, Dominic Maroh, Kevin Wimmer, Jonas Hector, Matthias Lehmann, Yannick Gerhardt (Bard Finne 55) Slawomir Peszko (Maurice Exslager 79), Daniel Halfar, Anthony Ujah (Kazuki Nagasawa 55), Patrick Helmes.

VfR Aalen: Jasmin Fejzic, Sascha Traut, Oliver Barth, Benjamin Hubner, Daniel Buballa, Andre Hainault, Nejmeddin Daghfous (Robert Lechleiste 64), Manuel Junglas (Leandro Grech 79), Andreas Hofmann, Enrico Valentini, Joel Pohjanpalo (Fabio Kaufmann 81).

Attendance: 45,700.

SG Faid II 4-2 SG Hambuch II

SUNDAY MORNING, and there is no better way to clear a beer clouded head than a stroll from the Gasthaus Fritzen to the FC Faid Sportplatz. And with the girls making their way into Cochem to pick up some gifts (while consuming cake and ice-cream) I'm freed up to watch a double header involving SG Faid and SG Hambuch. This is regional amateur football, although it has to be said the first team fixture was on par with any Essex Senior League encounter I've watched. The facilities too are impressive. Neat, tidy and supported by the local community with somewhere in the region of two hundred people adorning the touchline come the main event. But before that, Faid and Hambuch have a second team fixture to play out, and what it might lack in quality it more than

A big crowd at FC Faid.

makes up for in honest endeavour and drama. Faid are coached by a long-time friend of mine, Alexander Hein, last night he told me the team are struggling for numbers, I jovially inform him that my playing days are over, though I must admit I'm delighted to see he has a full complement as the temptation of one last game lingers long in the heart and mind, if not in the body. Thankfully, I'm able to take in the game from the touchline with my reporters pad and a Bitburger (well, when in Rome!).

Early exchanges are frantic, and it's not long before SG Faid's Marcel Koblenz finds space and fires past SG Hambuch keeper Sebastian Kramer to give the home side the lead. And midway through the opening period it's two. The unlucky Christian Wosnitza turning the ball into his own goal from close range. The visitor's rally, a Christopher Marx' strike is deflected past Faid keeper David Bracher, and Hambuch are back in the game.

The second half takes on the same pattern. The impressive Jens Rudolf head's home to extend Faid's advantage but Andre Kastre turn's in from close range to make it 3-2.

The game continues to ebb and flow, Faid's Kim Patrick Dohle is shown a second yellow card and sensing their chance, Hambuch swarm forward in search of a point saving goal. However, that man Rudolf has the final say, racing clear before beating Kramer with a low drive. Alexander is delighted at the end, "only for you Brian," he says to me as his elated charges leave the field.

SG Faid II: David Bracher, Dominik Sartoris, Norman Koblenz, Kim Patrick Dohle, Oliver Schneiders, Stephan Theisen, Jens Fiedermann, Marcel Koblenz, Jens Rudolf, Peter Targosz, Timo Schafer.

SG Faid II substitutes: Marco Prehn, Andreas Serwecinski, Alexander Hine, Myles Boldt, Kevin Hurter.

SG Hambuch II: Sebastian Kramer, Jan Schmitz, Lukas Schlaf, Luca Reichert, Michael Geyer, Thomas Schmitz, Christopher Marx, Andreas Laubenthal, Wale Nachiev, Andre Kastre, Christian Wosnitza.

SG Hambuch II substitutes: Michael Schmitz, Dennis Batta, Carsten Ternes.

Attendance: Small, but enthusiastic!

SG Faid 5-1 SG Hambuch

THE CROWD has sizably developed to around the two hundred mark as SG Faid and their SG Hambuch counterparts take the field. Before the game I bumped into 26-year old striker Luca Feldhausen, I'm delighted to see him. I've watched the lad grow up, ever since he was a small child he was kicking a ball around the Sportplatz, dreaming of becoming a maverick goal machine, it seems symbolic that here he is leading the local teams attack although early promise suggested he could have perhaps played at an even higher level.

Brian and Bernd.

Early in the game the local prodigy show's he has lost none of his touch or eagerness, firing low into the corner past and extended Alexander Schaub to give SG Faid the lead. His enthusiastic raised arms celebration suggests that the lad still enjoys the game as he did when I first saw him kicking about as a kid.

SG Faid are generally enjoying the better of proceedings, but they are pegged back when Thomas Klippel beat Andre Diederichs to level the score, this after Benedikt Sprengier had picked him out with a slide rule pass.

Nonetheless, Luca was keen to put on a show. Before the break he sent a dipping free-kick in off the underside of the bar to restore the home sides advantage.

Sadly, that's where my German adventure ended. I had to leave the game at half-time to meet the girls and catch our flight home. However, I'm pleased to report that on my arrival back in Blighty, an ecstatic Luca had messaged to inform me he had scored three goals. Fabian Jahnen and Marc Risser had added two more as SG Faid ran out handsome 5-1 winners.

SG Faid I: Andre Diederichs, Michael Monch, Arian Amin, Jan Berdi, Frank Mendoza Vargas, Fabien Jahnen, Klaus Fahrenkrog, Luca Feldhausen, Jarek Serwecinski, Julian Holzknecht, Marc Risser.

SG Faid I substitutes: Mario Scheid, Marc Heinzen.

SG Hambuch I: Alexander Schaub, Benedikt Sprengier, Tobias Graf, Eric Schumacher, Daniel Stripling, Lars Wilbert, Thomas Klippel, David Fihrmann, Roman Klinkner, Matthias Becker, Sebastian Fortmann.

SG Hambuch I substitutes: Mark Sallach, Philipp Schaden.

Attendance: Approximately 200.

* * *

It had been a perfect weekend, Victoria had enjoyed relaxation and pampering (with cake and wine) while I had grabbed a health slice of the beautiful game. Although it had been a while since our previous visit, our German friends had received us as if we had been their only the week before. I must recommend a visit to 1 FC Koln to any football fan, and if you are in the Mosel region take in an SG Faid match at the Sportplatz followed by a beer at the Gasthaus Fritzen. Oh, and if you make down the mountain into Cochem, complete the perfect holiday by going to see Peter Rochulus at J Koll & Cie winery, tell him I sent you.

Many thanks to Peter Rochulus, Bernd Pauly, Elizabeth Pauly, Jane Pauly, Katrin Pauly, Pascal Fritzen, Rainer Fritzen and Leanne McBeth along with all our friends in Faid for a wonderful weekend.

PAUL REANEY
— MASTER OF DISGUISE!

HOWEVER SUCCESSFUL the career of Paul Reaney might have turned out, he will be remembered as part of the Leeds United team humiliated by Colchester's 'Dads Army' team of 1971. Despite always being 'there or thereabouts' when the trophies were dished out, Leeds defeat at Layer Road that fateful February afternoon has over time become etched in FA Cup folk law and will haunt the players who wore the famous white shirts as well as their supporters forever.

Nevertheless, as if being turned over by a team four divisions lower isn't enough; one wonders how Reaney must have felt a few years later seeing his caricature in the 'Score' football annual of 1976?

The tough Leeds defender featured with a number of other First Division stars including Stanley Bowles, Peter Osgood, Malcolm MacDonald and John Toshack in the annuals quiz section titled 'Guess Who?'

The players had been made over with a series of crudely drawn hairstyles, beards, moustaches and spectacles, the reader's task simply to identify the footballer in question. In an age before political correctness, Reaney (pictured below, bottom right) somewhat alarmingly appears to have been disguised as leader of the Third Reich, Adolf Hitler!

Between 1964 and 1978, Paul Reaney became a permanent fixture in the Elland Road side. After making his debut during the 1963/64 Second Division championship season he would go on to make a hugely impressive 745 appearances for Leeds, adding success in the League, League Cup, FA Cup and Fairs Cup along with three international caps for England.

After Leeds, Reaney would play a further 38 games for neighbours Bradford City before finishing his career in Australia with Newcastle KB United.

Fulham born, Reaney was acknowledged by none other than George Best as the only player who could do a proper marking job on him. Despite playing in Don Revie's United team which met with widespread hatred, to my knowledge he had nothing to do with any invasion of mainland Europe!

WORLD CUP 2014
– BRAZIL (GROUP A)

It's here. Christmas and Birthdays have all come at once for everyone in the Jeeves' household, well almost everyone!

Brian reporting from the sofa.

Brazil 3–1 Croatia

A QUICK LAST MINUTE CHECK. TV remote commandeered (much to the wife's disgust), Panini sticker album coming along nicely (it's for the kids, honestly!), new England shirt purchased (I've gone for the late 70's retro version and not the overpriced garbage once again being served up by Nike). I've even acquired the official Brazil 2014 football, just to give our garden replays a little extra authenticity, oh, and finally, choice of beers for the opening match, Stella Artois.

Yep, the 2014 World Cup is upon us and despite morale in good old Blighty being slightly underwhelming, I for one fully intend to live, breath, eat and sleep every minute of it!

I'm additionally excited for this tournament because it's the first time my kids have collectively taken a real interest. Alfie has been football daft all his life, following me to every far-flung corner of the country supporting Southend United, whereas Stanley, despite an awful lot of brainwashing, is a relatively new fan. He supports Manchester City (because they won the league) and has

The Jeeves' World Cup team.

embraced the entire World Cup folly wholeheartedly. Indeed, on performing a recent school run I was alarmed to see Stan at the hub of a Panini sticker trading war with a clutch of other kids. This was far different to my day, you remember, when a 'shiny' was worth two of any other card, this was brutal with cards exchanging hands at a rate of knots and various arguments ensuing as to the value of Messi, Rooney and Stan's favourite City players Sergio Aguero and Joe Hart. Voices were raised and tempers were strained, this was real and no one was giving an inch!

Even our 4-year old, Oliver is in on it all, although his bold prediction that Southend will conclude the tournament as world champions suggests he still needs some educating. Still, with a lifetime of anguish ahead of him, I think it's only right on this occasion to let him, and our beloved Shrimpers, wallow in his misguided beliefs.

Nevertheless, you can't keep all of the people happy all of the time. This is going to be a difficult month for the lady in our lives, my wife Victoria. As kick-off draws ever closer, she buries her head in the Times supplement, occasionally (and somewhat annoyingly) popping up from the paper to delivery some dialogue from the pages within. Of course, any other time (except during a live televised game or Match of the Day) I'd nod and sound interested, sometimes I'll even give my own point of view on the topic, but right now all she receives is a distorted grunt of disapproval, she buries her head back in the magazine.

Concluding pre-match analysis and another beer is forfeited for a quick kick about with the kids in the garden. We play out our own version of the opening match. Of course, I didn't get to be Brazil, and only an inventive 'loan' which saw Cristiano Ronaldo (aka Stanley) able to swap Portugal for Brazil, prevented an impromptu bout of fisticuffs. Well, they can't all be Neymar can they! Anyhow, the usual 'next goal wins' see's Brazil grab a 5-4 success, there'll be plenty of time for revenge over the coming weeks.

The game gets under way amidst a yellow wave of optimism and expectation, however, it's Croatia who make the bolder start. David Luiz has to be alert after an Olic foray down the left, then the impressive Olic out jumped Dani Alves but was unable to direct his header past Julio Cesar following Perisic's testing centre. Brazil look wobbly, and soon the visitors stun not only the home crowd but most of the planet by grabbing the lead. Real Madrid's Luca Modric delivered a honey of a cross and the unlucky Marcello agonisingly diverted the ball past Cesar and into his own net. Brazil are all at sea and you can even feel the shockwaves here in the Essex Riviera!

The goal has stunned the kids too. "Brazil will still win, *won't* they dad?" Alfie asks inquisitively but the famous yellow shirts that have so often thrilled fans across the globe, today seem to be filled by charlatans. You know, the sort who I've seen turning out for an out of sorts Southend United on a wet Wednesday night at Grimsby or Darlington, a team who don't seem to know each other let alone how to win. I'm unable to give Alf a conclusive answer, he seems concerned.

There was further concern for the hosts when Neymar clashed with Modric. Japanese whistler Yuichi Nishimura produced a yellow card with the Croatian entourage displeased that Brazil's golden boy didn't receive a sterner punishment.

Brazil were still looking off-colour, but they start to make inroads towards the Croatian goal. Neymar and Fred are inches away from Oscar's cross while visitor's custodian Pletikosa is forced to block from Paulinho and then soon after from Oscar, this after sterling work from Neymar on the by-line. The tide had turned. Neymar will hit the ball far sweeter in his career but that mattered very little as his effort beat Pletikosa and found the net via the inside of an upright, sending a nation into hysteria in the process.

After the interval one would have expected Brazil to kick into gear, however, there passing is still uncharacteristically loose and there is a hesitant awkwardness about them. But then came the flashpoint that would overshadow all that had gone before, and indeed after it. Some call it part of the modern game. Fred falls theatrically under pressure from Lovren and referee Nishimura has no hesitation in pointing to the spot. Like I said, some call it part of the game, I certainly hope my watching kids don't adopt these tactics into their fledgling game as I consider it cheating!

Neymar dispatches the resulting penalty, just! Pletikosa got both mits to the ball and will perhaps be disappointed that he failed to restore a bit of justice!

Needless to say, Brazil's tails are up. Luiz heads over from Oscar's delicious centre while Neymar's flag kick is knocked on by Fred but falls wayward.

Croatia refuse to throw in the towel and once again seem to be hard done by. Perisic found the net after Olic had challenged Cesar, but his effort is bizarrely chalked off. Soon after, Modric's long range strike is scooped away by the Brazilian keeper. Croatia are having a right go but it's all to no avail. Perisic's shot is awkwardly kept out by Cesar, the hosts break swiftly, Oscar shakes of the shackles of Corluka before prodding past Pletikosa to put the result beyond doubt. The goal is well received in different circles. Brazilian fans are delirious, my kids are enthralled and Victoria is delighted to regain the TV remote, albeit briefly. The World Cup is well and truly underway and whether you like it or not we've got 63 games to go!

Brazil: Julio Cesar, Dani Alves, Thiago Silva, Luiz, Marcelo, Paulinho, Gustavo, Hulk, Oscar, Neymar, Fred.

Brazil substitutes: Jefferson, Fernandinho, Dante, Maxwell, Henrique, Ramires, Hernanes, Willian, Bernard, Jo, Maicon, Victor.

Croatia: Pletikosa, Srna, Corluka, Lovren, Vrsaljko, Modric, Rakitic, Perisic, Kovacic, Olic, Jelavic.

Croatia substitutes: Zelenika, Pranjic, Vukojevic, Schildenfeld, Brozovic, Rebic, Sammir, Vida, Eduardo, Subasic.

Referee: Yuichi Nishimura (Japan).

WORLD CUP 2014
— ITALY (GROUP D)

Football's coming home (from a night at the pub with the wife).

Brian from his usual spot.

England 1–2 Italy

USUAL SPOT SECURED: far left of the sofa, just off centre to the TV. Shirt selected: the controversial grey number worn at Euro 96 sporting 'Pearce 3' on the back. My, err, sorry the kids, Panini collection is stuttering somewhat. I've got Julian Draxler three times and still crave the Switzerland 'shiny'. Finally, choice of beer: Coors light (already had a reasonable early session at the boozer with Victoria). I'm pumped with hope and expectation (along with several Guinness's) and I'm about as ready as I ever could be, I just hope the England players are too!

Of course, I've no doubt their preparation has been every bit as military as that of my own, but in all seriousness I want this particular England team to prove the doubters wrong. If ever there was a case for the saying, "Don't blame the players, blame the game," then this particular team are living proof. The Premiership has turned its back on home talent, both on the park and in the dugout, many fans are either over critical or simply don't care about the national team, in short we seem to have fallen out of love with the team in which we once showed such blind faith.

The appointment of Roy Hodgson as manager raised a few eyebrows, but let's look at the facts. He has a decent record at getting teams with limited resources to the finals of major tournaments, he led England to qualification without a defeat, and he has nurtured through the emerging talents of Adam Lallana, Ross Barkley, Raheem Sterling and John Stone, footballers who are now being gabbed as 'World class'. Indeed, in the case of Barkley, parallels to Paul Gascoigne have been drawn up, but anyway, I'm waffling.

Besides, England v Italy: The equation is very simple, a decent result for England and we'll start believing we can actually win the World Cup. Danny Welbeck will be regarded as "able to do a job" and in short, tomorrow's hangover (today by the time you read this) will be mildly bearable. Defeat and we revert back to a nation on the brink of political meltdown, our national team will be viewed in the same light as Bradford Park Avenue's 1969/70 team (apologies to all the 'Stan's' I know*), and the thought of another crap performance versus Uruguay, coupled with heavily drinking anything over 4% will see us reaching for a double cyanide as opposed to the Alka Seltzer!

Notwithstanding my early evening session, I still believe I have the stamina for what here in England is a late night. Nevertheless, there have been casualties. The boy's brave attempts to stay awake have succumbed, probably due to a lengthy game in the garden in which England pipped the Italian's 20-17. Bobby Moore, Tony Currie and Stan Bowles were amongst the England goal scorers while Mario Balotelli hit ten for the Azzurri!

The big news ahead of the tie is the exclusion of Italy's legendary goalkeeper and Captain Gianluigi Buffon, due to an injury. Many see this as a boost to England, but personally, I'd rather see him in action, after all this is the World Cup and we should all want to see the best talent on display.

England make a decent start, Sterling teases the Azzurri rear-guard before sending a thundering effort into the side netting. The beer goggles told me it was a goal as I leapt out of the chair, the wife (who had lagged behind with a couple of ciders) was quick to inform me that it wasn't.

Soon after England were pressing again. Liverpool's Jordan Henderson drew a smart save from stand-in custodian Sirigu while Danny Welbeck fired another strike wayward.

Despite the good start England were mindful of the danger Italy possessed. Matteo Darmian was causing problems with his foray's down the flank while an irresistible Andrea Pirlo was conducting the orchestra as only he does best. The Azzurri displayed further their own intent as Joe Hart was forced into an unorthodox save to keep out Antonio Candreva's fizzing strike. But at this stage, England were still asking the lion's share of the questions. Skipper Steven Gerrard and Sterling almost forged an opportunity for Welbeck. Then, the Manchester United man almost picked out Daniel Sturridge, after displaying some terrific footwork, the anguish for those not asleep on our sofa was clearly evident.

Nevertheless, if you don't press home your advantage then you shouldn't be surprise when it bites you on the arse, and

Sleepy.

despite the continuous references to the aging Azzurri team, their dentures could still deliver a nasty nip. And so it proved, a short corner routine, straight off the training ground, arrived at Claudio Marchisio who in turn beat Hart with a honey of a strike. It was a shock to England's system, but you had to admire the skill and technique of the Juventus legend.

However, this England side are made of sterner stuff these days. Rooney raced down the left before picking out Sturridge with a delicious centre, the Liverpool man couldn't miss, Italy's lead had lasted little more than ninety seconds.

Italy finished the opening period the stronger. Darmian was off target after cutting in from a wide position, while the irrepressible Balotelli lifted over Hart but Jagielka was on the line to save the day.

There was a tactical change during the interval. Coors was subbed for a strong coffee as my eyelids became ever heavier, England too looked as if they had turned to the Brazilian beans as Sirigu produced another quality save to deny Sturridge in the first action of the second half. But before they could settle into a rhythm, England were chasing again. Candreva whipped in a great ball from the right and Balotelli arrived at the far post to nod past Hart and restore the Italian advantage.

England toiled. Rooney was wayward after a marauding run, while Welbeck was just off target after finding some room amidst the stifling Italian defence.

England continued to press. Rooney should have done better after Leighton Baines had picked him out, then the introduction of Barkley almost drew dividends only for Sirigu to palm away his low drive.

In the burning embers it was clear that England desperately needed some inspiration, meanwhile, reporting from the sofa I require a double shot of 'espresso pro-plus' to see the game to its conclusion.

Italy finished the game strongly. Pirlo's wonderful dead-ball effort bamboozled Hart but crashed off the woodwork, while Gary Cahill produced a great saving tackle as Ciro Immobile shaped to shoot.

With Costa Rica shocking Uruguay 3-1, Group D is still very open.

England had performed reasonably well, and looked more of a threat after the introduction of Lallana and Barkey. However, we lacked a bit of quality in the final third and question marks will be raised whether Roy Hodgson should persist with Rooney. All eyes are now on Thursday's clash with Uruguay, but in the meantime, it's goodnight from me, and it's long since been goodnight from them, zzzzzzzzzzz.

England: Joe Hart, Glen Johnson, Gary Cahill, Phil Jagielka, Leighton Baines, Steven Gerrard, Ross Henderson, Wayne Rooney, Raheem Sterling, Danny Welbeck, Daniel Sturridge.

England Substitutes: Frank Lampard, Ben Foster, James Milner, Fraiser Forster, Adam Lallana, Rickie Lambert, Jack Wilshere, Chris Smalling, Phil Jones, Ross Barkley, Luke Shaw.

Italy: Salvatore Sirigu, Giorgio Chiellini, Matteo Darmian, Antonio Candreva, Claudio Marchisio, Mario Balotelli, Andrea Barzagli, Daniele De Rossi, Gabriel Paletta, Andrea Pirlo, Marco Verratti.

Italy Substitutes: Thiago Motta, Lorenzo Insigne, Marco Parolo, Alberto Aquilani, Antonio Cassano, Alessio Cerci, Leonardo Bonucci, Mattia Perin, Ignazio Abate, Gianluigi Buffon, Mattia De Sciglio, Ciro Immobile.

Referee: Bjorn Kuipers (Netherlands).

* 'Stan's' is a nickname given to Bradford Park Avenue fans after a character called 'Boring Stan the Avenue fan', created by Tony Hanann, a supporter of rivals Bradford City for the fanzine "Bernard of the Bantams".

WORLD CUP 2014 (GROUP D)
OUT OF LUCK AND LOW ON BEER!
Brian reporting from the sofa.

Uruguay 2-1 England

OK, THIS IS BLOODY IMPORTANT NOW! Usual sofa seat secured. Shirt selected: The 'Gazza Italia 90' number with 19 on the back. Choice of beer: Running low, so several bottles of Bitburger which were left over from the Germany v Portugal game. My Panini book (yep mine, no use covering it up anymore) has made steady progress. Lukas Podolski has been added while Joe Hart was shamelessly 'lifted' from my 7-year-old son Stanley's swaps while he was sleeping (I told him the tooth fairy took it). As for tonight's match, I'm as fired up for Uruguay as Ray 'Butch' Wilkins was that night in Montevideo back in 1984, when as part of a lacklustre England team trailing 2-0 he fervently requested, "Give me that fuckin' ball," which wasn't just heard by the targeted fledgling ball boy, but by an entire audience watching back home on live TV, funny how you remember things like that!

Our pre-match garden kick-about saw a resounding victory for England. Once again the opposition was reinforced, this time due to the boy's lack of Uruguayan knowledge. Lionel Messi joined Luis Suarez in attack and briefly La Celeste held an advantage. However, a "dinner's on the table" shout from Victoria in the kitchen resulted in a quick-fire goal-glut from the Three Lions. Stanley Matthews grabbed a hat trick and five from new cap Ronnie Pountney (my all-time favourite Southend United player) gave England an unassailable

Goal!

lead. As the smell of cod 'n' chips grew ever stronger, David Beckham and Geoff Hurst found the net to secure a 10-4 triumph, giving me and the boys just enough time to wolf down the fish supper before kick-off, perfect.

Despite a defeat last time out to Italy, there has been an unusual air of positivity surrounding England. Raheem Sterling's display was hugely encouraging as was the sight of Ross Barkley scampering at the Azzurri back line. The only real question mark is over Rooney, does Roy Hodgson stick or twist? Meanwhile, Uruguayans were concerned over talisman Suarez' troublesome knee, which threatened to disrupt his tournament.

Many people have installed the South Americans as favourites for this particular tie. However, as proved, nothing is certain in this World Cup, already I've seen both Spain and Portugal imitate the Southend United team I watched haplessly humped 8-1 at Gillingham in 1987 and Uruguay's display against Costa Rica wasn't much better. I'm confident that England can win this one. In the words from Ron Greenwood's 1982 squads World Cup song, I believe, "*This time, we'll get it right*".

But the first forty-five minutes prove to be infuriatingly frustrating for England. A slip from Muslera almost lets in Sturridge but the Uruguay keeper recovered in the nick of time, while at the other end a Suarez flag-kick almost deceived Hart at his near post.

The teams continue to spar. Rooney's bending free-kick was inches away with Muslera rooted to the spot then Uruguay went even closer as Rodrigu's thundering effort flashed across the face of goal with Hart fully extended.

After Cavani struck over from Suarez' corner, England went mighty close to grabbing the lead when Rooney's close range header clattered the bar, you have to wonder what the Manchester United man has to do to find a goal in the World Cup Finals.

Nevertheless, that aside, England were struggling to make any real headway and Uruguay sensed their chance. Cavarni's exquisite centre picked out Suarez who slipped the attentions of Jagielka and headed beyond Hart. It was a dagger in the heart for England, but an unsurprising source of the pain.

England looked for an immediate response. Sturridge raced onto Rooney's slide rule pass but Muslera fisted aside.

England continued to labour, but showed very little in the way of a potent goal threat and were nowhere near the standards they had set previously against Italy.

During the interval a Panini swapping mission ensues between me and Stanley. He seems happy to have acquired the England 'shiny', though with bedtime imminent, his Nerf gun is locked and loaded, I'm well aware that he is more than ready for any further medalling from the tooth fairy.

England started the second period sluggishly. Hart turned aside Suarez' deflected corner, then the talismanic Liverpool front man proved he's human by firing horribly high and wide after finding himself some room. Cavani almost doubled La Celeste advantage, but side footed wide after getting behind the English backline.

England had rode their luck and were keen to make the most of it. Rooney showed great control to craft an opportunity from Baines low centre, but Muslera was once again equal to the effort.

England were flagging and looked short of ideas, it was hoped that the introduction of Barkley and Lallana might inject some impetus into the performance. But the lacklustre nature of the recital continued to show little of the fluidity displayed in the opening game against the Italian's.

However, it takes just a second for a game to turn on its head. Johnson wriggled down the right flank before sending over a delicious centre, this time Rooney couldn't miss, much to the delight of the pockets of England fans scattered around the ground.

England suddenly had a spring in their step. The impressive Muslera pushed away a Sturridge effort, now it was Uruguay who were on the ropes.

But Uruguay still had a fighter capable of delivering the knockout punch. Gerrard misjudged the flight of a long punt forward, Suarez didn't need any further invitation to race clear and fire past a marooned Hart to restore the South American's advantage.

In the burning embers England pressed in vain, but it was to no avail. It's going to take a snooker of monumental proportions to see the Three Lions progress further in this World Cup, clearly the structure of our game has to change.

Disappointed, disenchanted, disillusioned this whole experience has left me both physically and emotionally drained. I desperately need some kip, besides, right now I pretty much hate football …eh, what's that you said Japan v Greece at 11pm …oh, go on then…

Uruguay: Muslera, Caceres, Gimenez, Godin, A. Pereira, Gonzalez, Rios, Lodeiro, Rodriguez, Cavani, Suarez.

Uruguay substitutes: Lugano, Fucile, Gargano, Hernández, Forlán, Stuani, Muñoz, Pérez, Ramírez, Coates, Silva.

England: Hart, Johnson, Cahill, Jagielka, Baines, Henderson, Gerrard, Sterling, Rooney, Welbeck, Sturridge.

England substitutes: Wilshere, Lampard, Smalling, Foster, Oxlade-Chamberlain, Jones, Milner, Lambert, Lallana, Barkley, Forster, Shaw.

Referee: Carlos Velasco Carballo (Spain).

WORLD CUP 2014 (GROUP D)
ENGLAND HUNG OUT TO DRY
Brian reporting from the Sofa.

Costa Rica 0-0 England

IT'S OFFICIAL, English football has been hung out to dry! The press are having a field day, and social media sites are awash with jokes and jibes about the players and teams we should all be so proud of. Even my kids are starting to question the presence of this particular England team at the World Cup. "If we're already out, why are we bothering to watch" Alfie asks inquisitively. I'll tell you why my lad, *BECAUSE WE BLOODY HAVE TO!*

Anyway, usual seat on the sofa secured, it's not been a particularly lucky vantage point to date. Nevertheless, through watching so much football of late, a deep gluteus maximus created groove has now provided me with an extremely comfortable place to park my arse. Although being stuck in my ways, I still believe 'football comfort' is at its premium when I "grin and bear it" on the old wooden East Stand seats at my beloved Southend United's Roots Hall Stadium.

My Panini book has made heady progress, mainly due to the fact I've finally succumbed to the cheat option and ordered all remaining 'needs' online. Stanley is none the wiser, but I suspect he smells a rat as I've given him all my remaining swaps for no apparent reason.

Tonight's, choice of beer: Carlsberg. Some might say a cheap and nasty option, but I have a bottle of gin on standby just in case it all gets too painful. The subtle blend of juniper berries and …err …other stuff has helped me through several laborious situations, although some tell me it acts as a depressant you know!

Shirt selection: In a bid to restore some faith and reminisce healthier epochs, I've gone for the Euro 96 home shirt. I still fondly remember witnessing that particular Lions team pip Spain at a passion filled Wembley with my mate Tony Long.

That game was the last time England won a penalty shootout. Lionhearted Stuart Pearce led a whole nation the way no politician could ever dream of, with a release of pure emotion after hammering his spot kick beyond Andoni Zubizarreta. Despite the almost inevitable defeat to Germany in the semi-final, the country were fervently devoted to what was regarded as one of the best teams we've produced since 1966, how times change!

Our pre-match garden kick about has taken on a somewhat farcical guise. Despite making a spectacular start to the *REAL* World Cup, the boys are less than enthusiastic about being Costa Rica due to the lack of household names. Therefore England locked horns with The Rest of the World, facing both Messi and Neymar of course. The contest is an entertaining one, with both Steve Coppell and Stanley Bowles grabbing a brace for the Three Lions, 'Stan' Messi bagged all four for the Rest of the World. The match is settled by a penalty shoot-out, unsurprisingly England lose.

Right, England versus Costa Rica. Pardon me if I start wondering off track a little, I've been reporting on a cricket match for the local newspaper this afternoon, any references to '*in the deep*' or '*slip catch*' are purely by accident as my brain is somewhat fried right now, although any exclamation sounding similar to 'whip his bails off' might, in this case, still be a reference to football!

Anyway, the nation is still reeling with many calling for Roy Hodgson to ring the changes. They are not to be disappointed with no less than nine new faces coming in to the starting line-up. Costa Rica have exceeded expectations at this tournament with notable victories over both Uruguay and Italy. The Central American's have long since lost the tag of whipping boys, indeed, just a point will see them deservedly top the group.

Early exchanges are untidy, with both sides passing wayward. Algerian referee Djamel Haimoudi wasn't helping the flow, seemingly liking the sound of his own whistle a little too much.

Joel Campbell's early effort is deflected wide by Gary Cahill, but its twelve minutes before we witness any form of meaningful effort at goal from England.

Stanley.

Daniel Sturridge firing just wide after Jack Wilshere's penetrating run had fashioned the opportunity. Soon after, the ever willing Sturridge fizzed over the bar, while Costa Rica went mighty close when Borges' dead ball strike was tipped onto the bar by Ben Foster.

England believed they should have had a penalty when Sturridge was felled by Duarte, but whistler Mr. Haimoudi is unmoved by pleas for a spot kick. I turn to Stanley and ask his thoughts on the game, "England are playing well, but the ref is dozy," was his response.

England are *enjoying* (if that's the correct wording) the better of proceedings. The energetic Ross Barkley was off target after a rare fluent passage of play, nevertheless, we reach half time on level terms after a steady if not spectacular performance.

During the interval a contractual argument ensues between me and the missus. Victoria firmly believes that England's World Cup demise would restore some kind of status quo regarding ownership of the TV remote. I inform her in no uncertain terms that she is way off the mark, thus the commencement of a three day silent protest. She leaves the room, I hear the door slam. At the moment Vic would rather go jogging in the pissing rain than watch the second half with me, I'll cook my own dinner then!

The second period proves to be flat and fairly lifeless. Sturridge is denied by Costa Rica keeper Navas and soon after slots agonisingly wide after a terrific interchange with Wilshere, the Liverpool man has to start taking these chances if he wants to be regarded as international class. Meanwhile, Costa Rica threaten, but Christian Bolanos' snapshot is expertly dealt with by Foster.

England introduce Gerrard and Rooney into the fray. The latter almost breaks the deadlock but Navas fingered his exquisite chip over the top. The encounter is little more than a training exercise now. Costa Rica are happy with a point while England seem simply content not to lose. The kids have lost interest, they have long since deserted me for the Xbox.

In the burning embers, Gerrard's deep free kick is inches away from a flying Rooney, but the final whistle brought very little in the way of restored pride. Roy Hodgson has a mammoth job, not only to turn around the team's fortunes but to re-establish faith nationwide.

Of course, this whole World Cup has been a disastrous experience for England players and fans alike. However, every cloud has a silver lining, at least I won't be stuck on hold for an hour when I phone to book our tickets for San Marino's visit to Wembley in October!

Costa Rica: 1-Keylor Navas; 16-Cristian Gamboa, 3-Giancarlo Gonzalez, 6-Oscar Duarte, 15-Junior Diaz, 19-Roy Miller; 17-Yeltsin Tejeda, 5-Celso Borges; 10-Bryan Ruiz; 9-Joel Campbell, 14-Randall Brenes.

Costa Rica substitutes: 2-Johnny Acosta, 4-Michael Umana, 7-Christian Bolanos, 8-Heiner Mora, 11-Michael Barrantes, 12-Waylon Francis, 13-Oscar Esteban Granados, 18-Patrick Pemberton, 20-Diego Calvo, 21-Marco Urena, 22-Jose Miguel Cubero, 23-Daniel Cambronero.

England: 13-Ben Foster 16-Phil Jones, 5-Gary Cahill, 12-Chris Smalling, 23-Luke Shaw; 17-James Milner, 8-Frank Lampard, 7-Jack Wilshere, 21-Ross Barkley, 20-Adam Lallana, 9-Daniel Sturridge.

England substitutes: 1-Joe Hart, 2-Glen Johnson, 3-Leighton Baines, 4-Steven Gerrard, 6-Phil Jagielka, 10-Wayne Rooney, 11-Danny Welbeck, 13-Ben Foster, 14-Jordan Henderson, 15-Alex Oxlade-Chamberlain, 18-Rickie Lambert, 19-Raheem Sterling.

Referee: Djamel Haimoudi (Algeria).

SUPER MARIO (STAN'S FIRST HEADLINE)

FIFA WORLD CUP FINAL

Brian reporting from the Sofa.

Germany 1-0 Argentina

And so, the end is near
And so I face, the final curtain...

SOMETHING LIKE THAT ANYWAY. It seems like only yesterday that me and the boys sat down, full of enthusiasm, to watch Brazil and Croatia open the twenty-first FIFA World Cup. And yet it's been a month and here we are, sat in the same place, acting out the final scene. Anyway, enough, here is the lowdown.

My Panini sticker album has long since been completed and is packed away until such time as I believe the kids should inherit it. Tonight's choice of shirt is an interesting one that takes me back to the World Cup heroes of my childhood. Though I am backing Germany, mainly due to the wonderful friends I made during my time playing there, tonight I'll be wearing a retro Cruyff 1974 Holland shirt, complete with the iconic number 14 on the back.

The 1974 World Cup Finals in Germany were the first I can recall intensely watching with my dad. Holland, despite losing to the hosts in the final, were indisputably the stars of the tournament, they had swagger and played the

Saved!

game in a way that captured my 5-year-old imagination the same way the likes of Messi and Neymar have done for my kids today. I couldn't wait for their games to come on our old black and white TV, nor to practise my fairly hopeless 'Cruyff turns' with the old man over the park. The fact they could entrance me before lamentably losing their bottle in the final (they did the same four years later in Argentina), in some haphazard way set me up for a lifetime of frustration following Southend United, with Johnny Rep and Johan Neeskens instead of Alan Little and Chris Guthrie of course.

Instead of a beer, tonight's beverage of choice is a bottle of Three Barrels brandy. I'm not sure if my thinking behind this selection is due to the grandeur of the event or the slight feeling of melancholy that has overcome most Englishmen on World Cup Final day since 1966, still, it's numbing any lingering pain and there's always next time of course!

Our pre-match garden foray is as competitive as ever. The boys take on the role of the Argentinian's while I simulate a legendary German team in which I'm able to fulfil the protagonists of both Bert Trautmann and Franz

Beckenbauer. As I'm approaching my 46th birthday, I realise that my playing days might be long gone by the next finals, therefore a harsh lesson is handed out to the boys as Germany, bizarrely playing in Dutch colours, romp to a 10-3 triumph with Trautmann even finding the time to leave the rigging to bag a hat trick. This might seem unforgiving to some of you, however, kids are resilient and besides, their time will come.

As we sit watching the pre-match build up, I think about how this World Cup has influenced the boys. Stanley has clearly been indoctrinated the most. He is still beautifully wet behind the ears with all this malarkey. Messi, Neymar and James (Rodriguez, not David) are his new mavericks, and he still spends hours in the garden playing out the Dutch's annihilation of Spain as well as finding the top corner over and over 'Messi style'. Nevertheless, where there's a yin there's a yang. He is still blissfully unaware of the traps that lie in wait for a fledgling supporter, and that for every Holland 5 Spain 1 there are a million piss-poor Southend 0 Bury 0's on a freezing Tuesday night in February and for every Messi and Neymar there are an endless conveyer belt of hapless Gordon Connelly's or Tesfaye Bramble's!

Stanley is without question the Jeeves family's 'grubby urchin', however, I've noticed of late he has been pillaging my Brylcreem by the handful in an attempt to add a bit of 'Neymar panache' to his usually scruffy barnet. Still, I can't talk, there are still photograph's floating around of yours truly with a Keegan style perm and just recently I had a go at growing Gerry Francis sideburns, footballers were proper elegant back then you know!

Anyway, in international football terms it doesn't get much bigger than Germany versus Argentina. The German's have without doubt been the outstanding team of the tournament, whereas the South American's possess the greatest current player on the face of the planet in the shape of maestro Messi.

The drama starts before a ball is kicked. Germany's Khedira is ruled out during the warm-up, his place going to Borussia Monchen-gladbach's Kramer.

Early exchanges are insipid, with the play condensed into the central area as both teams muscle for a grain of supremacy. Higuain fires across the face of goal with Neuer fully extended, while Argentina deal comfortably with a couple of Muller center's after the German's had swept down the right flank.

Genius Messi is struggling to make an impact, nevertheless, he shows Hummels a clean pair of heals to provide further evidence that his threat is ever present.

Then a golden opportunity. Kroos' back-header is woefully short, but Higuian pulls his shot horribly wide after finding himself one-on-one with Neuer.

Soon after Higuian believed he had broken the deadlock. Messi and Lavezzi manufactured the opening, only for a hawkeyed assistant to flag him off-side.

Just before the interval it's Germany's turn to feel the agony. Kroos flag-kick is met by the meat of Howedes forehead, only for his effort to cannon back off an upright. The German's anguish is evident, but they have little time to dwell, as Italian whistler Nicola Rizzoli sounds for half time.

When the teams re-emerge, one wonders if something sinister has been placed in Messi's half-time cuppa as the little prodigy races clear, beats Neuer, but is uncharacteristically off target. The German custodian is soon called upon to snub out the threat of Higuain, colliding heavily with the Napoli man in the process. And although Germany respond when Klose heads into Romero's gloves, the game has once again become wedged in the central area's with a series of niggling fouls cracking up the temperature a notch.

The teams continued to spar prudently. Schurrle was unable to profit from a fluent German build-up while Messi shot wayward after skipping past a couple of desperate challenges.

The lack of viable goalmouth action has seen the kids retreat to the garden for an all-stars kick about, however, as soon as the commentator's vocal tones become higher, they race back in front of the telly.

Inside the goggle-box, Messi slips clear but the German rear-guard mop up his low centre, this has been far from the classic many (except my mate Roy McDonough) predicted. The teams have largely cancelled each other out, as defenders swarm around anyone who gets so much as a sniff of goal.

Ninety minutes can't produce a winner so it's extra, or for the football crazy amongst us, bonus time!

Romero instinctively saved from Shurrle, while at the other end Palacio lifts the ball over Neuer only to watch it drift wide.

But with time running, out came the golden moment that crystalized the whole occasion. Schurrle picked out Mario Gotze with an exquisite centre, and the young Bayern Munich midfielder beat Romero with a crisp finish. Sure, there have been better World Cup goals, but it's the one my kids will remember the most, just as I recall sitting with my old man watching Gerd Muller settle the 1974 final.

The final whistle produces the usual tears and celebrations. Everyone will take something from this World Cup. Some will cherish it while others will spark criticism and revolt. Nonetheless, together, me and the boys have collected stickers, played out titanic encounters in the garden, been dazzled by Messi, despaired by England, wooed by the Dutch and gobsmacked as Brazil had their pants pulled down by the German's. They have been able to watch each game and choose the county they favour based on player worship as opposed to administrative lunacy concocted by the political madmen (and women) who have made peace on this planet such a fragile commodity, football has brought us all closer together.

And so to the final act. Me and the boys look on as the Jules Rimet trophy is presented to the elated German skipper Philipp Lahm, meanwhile here in our small corner of Shoeburyness, Essex, England the TV remote is handed back to the other side of the sofa to my somewhat flustered wife Victoria. Normal service is resumed for the time being… Roll on the Euro's in France 2016!

Germany: Neuer, Lahm, Boateng, Hummels, Howedes, Khedira, Schweinsteiger, Muller, Kroos, Ozil, Klose.

Germany substitutes: Zieler, Grosskreutz, Ginter, Schurrle, Podolski, Draxler, Durm, Mertesacker, Gotze, Kramer, Weidenfeller.

Argentina: Romero, Zabaleta, Demichelis, Garay, Rojo, Biglia, Mascherano, Perez, Higuain, Messi, Lavezzi.

Argentina substitutes: Orion, Campagnaro, Gago, Di Maria, Rodriguez, Augusto Fernandez, Federico Fernandez, Palacio, Alvarez, Aguero, Basanta, Andujar.

Referee: Nicola Rizzoli (Italy).

A WORKING MAN'S GAME

We've come to stand on terrace steps
Have waited all week long
From mines and yards and factory floors
We stand and sing our songs

Our working week has led to this
Of nothing else, we talk
With scarf and rattle out the door
To football ground we walk

Last week's loss is in the past
The team were awful then
But seven days have since gone by
They're heroes once again

A pre-match beer, the turnstile clicks
We've just arrived in heaven
"Why's he playing him in goal?"
The new boy wears eleven

The urban flow, the anxious crowd
Emotions wild and free
Our wages blown on "not so greats"
Who fill our hearts with glee

Out the blue, a late, late goal
A tingle down the spine
He couldn't hit a door last week
Today he's been sublime

Post match beers go down so well
As do the cod 'n' chips
They'll win the cup the words ring round
Straight from the masses lips

We trudge back to the factory floors
The yards and down the mines
And talk about the match in depth
All experts stood on lines

Weather we've won, drawn or lost
The fact it still remains
Try, as you will soulless millionaires
THIS IS STILL A WORKING MANS GAME!

THE GRIM CHAIRMAN – FOOTBALL REAPER

You say our club is dying
Our future lies away
A futuristic stadium
It's what will save the day

A castle made of breezeblocks
Our history is lost
You tell us that its progress
We ask you, "at what cost"

Our real home demolished
Raised into the ground
The fans they stand and protest
You never hear a sound

Everywhere to nowhere
Stuck outside the town
"Football Club de Comatose"
And now we're going down

We drop with haste, a led balloon
Now our club is gone
An ugly store stands on the site
Where once our favourites shone

But if you ever get the chance
You'd do it all again
'Coz killing off great football clubs
It's what has made your name.

RIP the clubs and grounds lost to greed.

POST OFFICE
FIELD OF DREAMS

*Inspired by my son Stanley, who switched off the iPad to go
and have a proper kick about, my big mate Ed who almost
shed a tear at the sight of a discarded football at the side of
the North Circular, and my childhood playing field, now a
assemblage of ugly shops and flats.*

*A tatty ball lies in the kerb,
flat and somewhat rough
A load of kids, they left it here,
once they'd had enough.*

*In days gone by, this handsome sphere
was kicked around the park
The kids arrived at 8am
and played till it was dark.*

*Every evening after school,
we'd chase about the grass
Kick the ball between the coats
or smash a greenhouse glass!*

I've played against some legends,
like Moore and Hurst and Law
We picked our teams and in our dream,
'twas their shirts we wore.

Now the park is built upon,
bricks crush childhood dreams
The ball is gone and brains are fried
by pixelated screens.

No more jumpers down for goal
as great games are replayed
Council greed, they count their cash
as ugly bricks are laid.

The place we played those mighty games,
a hundred on each side
Is now placed firmly in the past
as more real football dies.

Now where's the camaraderie
from games upon the green
Wii and Xbox just won't win,
there ain't no 'I' in team!

WE'LL NEVER WALK ALONE!

Brian reminds football supporters that it's much more than just a game.

TWO SUCCESSIVE DEFEATS have somewhat dampened the early season optimism amongst my fellow Southend United supporters. Nevertheless, here is a timely reminder what football is all about. Those priceless days spent in the stands or on the terraces are something we should treasure; they are about passion, friendship, camaraderie. With the blessing of his family, I share the piece I wrote for my friend Martin Cranmer. However good or bad Southend United might be, what I'd give to spend another afternoon at the match with him.

It's 4:40pm some Saturday afternoon in the future, we're 49-miles North of Northshire and Southend United are losing 3-0.

Our fate was sealed quite early in the match. The finger of blame has long since been pointed at the players, manager, chairman, bus driver and what's more it's now pissing with rain and we've got a 5-hour journey home!

In one final act of defiance the travelling Shrimpers burst into a chorus of, "Oh Southend we love you," because despite what has been a bloody awful 90-minutes on the terraces, we do.

In some unique way, this seems to unite our travelling band, making it all worthwhile. Of course those who see the result in Sunday's paper won't understand, "Waste of money," or "Why bother," they'll say. Nevertheless, this single act of solidarity is something only the few who do it will appreciate.

I think back to the numerous times we've stood together, miles from home, win, lose or draw, rain, shine or snow and think of you.

You can't be seen but I know you're here, kicking every ball, cheering every goal, sinking a cheeky pint.

I turn back to the match, it's 4-0 now, but it doesn't matter, we'll be doing it again next week and you'll be there too.

It has been four years since God found something far more important for you to do, but we still love and remember you and know we will never walk alone.

Sleep tight my friend.

Martin Cranmer
26th March 1970 – 6th August 2010

The author would like to thank the following people who showed their faith by pre-ordering this publication – thank you.

Alan Adair	Luton Town
Feb Anene	Chelsea
Mary Anene	Chelsea
Altan Ali	Southend United
Andrew Barr	Clapton FC
Trevor Bashford	Southend United
Steven Batchelor	Southend United
Ian Bentley	Liverpool
Kathy Bloom	Chelsea
Dave Brabbing	Southend United
Andy Brace	Colchester United
Daryl Brough	England
Richard Brown	Southend United
James Browne	West Ham United
Karl Burgess	Liverpool
Tony & Ken Canham	West Ham United
Lesley Catchpowle	Charlton Athletic
Carl Catley	Manchester United
Brian Chester	Aston Villa
Peter Coster	Southend United
Mark Cox	Arsenal
Phil Cox	Southend United
Zoe Cranmer	Southend United
Robert Craven	Southend United
Steve Dare	Arsenal
Rob Davies	Millwall
Jenny Davies	Southend United
Jo Denton	Southend United
Frank Dixon	Newcastle United
Peter Dorrell	Arsenal
Peter Dudley	Norwich City
Alan Drew (R.I.P.)	Portsmouth
Sam Eades	Liverpool
Glen Eckett	Canvey Island
Mark Edwards	The Real Clapton
Michael Eyre	Walsall
Jordan Fredrick	Southend United
Groyney	Glasshoughton Welfare

Doreen Hague	Southend United & Huddersfield Town
Kevin Hall	West Ham United
Wayne Harris	Southend United
Rob Heys	Accrington Stanley
Claire Houghton	Southend United
Lorraine Huckle	West Ham United
Matt Hudson	Colchester United
Neil Irvine	Leyton Orient
Ken Jarvis	Southend United
Eileen Jeeves	Southend United
Tina Jones	Walsall
Peter Kadesh	Southend United
Terry Kenton	West Ham United
Stuart Leslie	Liverpool
Tony Long	West Ham United
Steve Lovell	Chelsea
Kelvin Luxton	Southend United
Nick Mackie	Southend United
Paul Marshall	Southend United
Don Martin	Walsall
Roy McDonough	Ex-Southend, Colchester and Walsall
Sally Midlane	Charlton Athletic
Chris Mills	Ipswich Town
Gary Moss	Tottenham Hotspur
Helen Mulley & James Partridge	Lexden Saints Under 10's
Mary Parry	Ipswich Town
James Partridge & Helen Mulley	Lexden Saints Under 10's
Nigel Perkins	Southend United
Ashley Perry	West Ham United
Scott Peters	Southend United
Chris Phillips	Southend United
Neal Phillips	Southampton
Darren Posnack	Southend United
Lou & Lee Purnell	Aston Villa

Royston Randle	Walsall	Ian Stokes	West Ham United
Derek Reeves	Wormatia Worms	Nicola Stott	Southend United
Ian Reis	Millwall	Andre'a Sturniolo	Liverpool
Luis Reis	Southampton	Ken Taylor	Southend United
Keith Roe	Southend United	Darren Thurley	Southend United
Frank Sanders	Arsenal	Enrico Tiritera	Tottenham Hotspur
Keith Shields	West Ham United		& Lazio
Sam Shilvock	Aston Villa	Sheila Turnnidge	Southend United
Andy Sims	Canvey Island	Andy Ward	Southend United
Adam Sloan	Rangers	Charly Watson	Southend United
Andy Smith	Concord Rangers	Susan Watts	Hibernian
April Smith	Southend United	Mark Westwick	West Ham United
Richard Smith	Southend United	Ashley Wilkopp	Tottenham Hotspur
Baiju Solanki	Southend United	Lee Wittridge	Tottenham Hotspur
	& Tottenham Hotspur	Steve Wolfendale	Southend United
Bradley Star	Manchester United	Daniel Wright	Arsenal
Robert Star	Manchester United		
Paul Stevens	West Ham United	Jon Varney	Liverpool

Colchester United v Wolverhampton Wanderers
by Stanley Jeeves.